SHELLEY, GODWIN, AND THEIR CIRCLE

BY
H. N. BRAILSFORD

ARCHON BOOKS
1969

First Published 1913
Reprinted 1969 by arrangement with
Oxford University Press
in an unaltered and unabridged edition

SBN: 208 00751 2
Library of Congress Catalog Card Number: 69-13624
Printed in the United States of America

CONTENTS

CHAPTER		PAGE
I	THE FRENCH REVOLUTION IN ENGLAND	7
II	THOMAS PAINE	56
III	WILLIAM GODWIN AND THE REVOLUTION	78
IV	"POLITICAL JUSTICE"	94
V	GODWIN AND THE REACTION	142
VI	GODWIN AND SHELLEY	168
VII	MARY WOLLSTONECRAFT	186
VIII	SHELLEY	212
	BIBLIOGRAPHY	252
	INDEX	255

SHELLEY, GODWIN, AND THEIR CIRCLE

CHAPTER I

THE FRENCH REVOLUTION IN ENGLAND

THE history of the French Revolution in England begins with a sermon and ends with a poem. Between that famous discourse by Dr. Richard Price on the love of our country, delivered in the first excitement that followed the fall of the Bastille, and the publication of Shelley's *Hellas* there stretched a period of thirty-two years. It covered the dawn, the clouding and the unearthly sunset of a hope. It begins with the grave but enthusiastic prose of a divine justly respected by earnest men, who with a limited horizon fulfilled their daily duties in the city. It ends in the rapt vision, the magical music of a singer, who seemed as he sang to soar beyond the range of human ears. The hope passes from the confident expectation of instant change, through the sobrieties of disillusionment and the recantations of despair, to the iridescent dreams of a future which has taken wing and made its home in a fairy world.

In 1789 when Dr. Price preached to his ardent congregation of Nonconformist Radicals in the meeting-house at the Old Jewry, the prospect was definite and the place of the millennium was merely the England over which George III. ruled. The hope was a robust but pedestrian " mental traveller," and its limbs wore the precise garments of political formulæ. It looked for honest Parliaments and manhood suffrage, for the triumph of democracy and the abolition of war. Its scene as Wordsworth put it, was

> Not in Utopia, subterraneous fields,
> Or some secreted island, Heaven knows where,
> But in the very world which is the world
> Of all of us, the place where in the end
> We find our happiness, or not at all.

The impetus of its own aspiration carried it swiftly beyond the prosaic demand for Parliamentary Reform. It evolved its programme for the reconstruction of all human institutions, and projected the amendment of human nature itself. America had made

THE FRENCH REVOLUTION 9

an end of kings and France was in the full tide of revolution. Nothing was too mighty for this new-begotten hope, and the path to human perfectibility stretched as plain as the narrow road to Bunyan's Heavenly City.

There followed the phase when persecution from alarmed defenders of things as they are, disgust at the failures of the revolution in France, and contempt for the futilities of the revolution at home, drove the new movement into as many refuges as its votaries had temperaments. For some there was cynicism, for others recantation. " The French Revolution " as Hazlitt put it, " was the only match that ever took place between philosophy and experience ; and waking from the trance of theory we hear the words Truth, Reason, Virtue, Liberty, with the same indifference or contempt that a cynic who has married a jilt or a termagant listens to the rhapsodies of lovers." Godwin found his own alluring by-way, and turning away at once from political repression and political agitation, became the pioneer of philosophic anarchism. To Shelley at the end of this marvellous thirty years of ardour, speculation, and despair, the hope became winged. She had her place no longer in " the very world which is the world of all of us." She had moved to

> Kingless continents, sinless as Eden
> Around mountains and islands inviolably
> Prankt on the sapphire sea.

It requires no inordinate effort for us who live in an equable political climate to realise the atmosphere of Dr. Price's Old Jewry sermon. The lapse of a century indeed has made him a more intelligible figure than he could have seemed to the generation which immediately followed him. He was temperate in his rationalism and thrifty in his philanthropy. He tended to Unitarianism in his theology, but was a sturdy defender of Free Will. He had written a widely-read apology for the Colonial side in the American Civil War. A stout individualist in his political theory, inspired, as were nearly all the English progressive thinkers of his day, by an extreme jealousy of State action, he yet guarded himself carefully against anarchical conclusions, and followed Saint Paul in teaching obedience to magistrates. He had written a treatise on ethics which on some points anticipated Kant. But his most characteristic pre-occupation was a study of finance in the interests of national thrift and social benevolence. This cold moralist, who despised the emotional aspects of human nature and found no place for the affections in his scheme of the virtues, lapsed into passion when he attacked the National Debt, and developed an arithmetical enthusiasm when he explained his plan for providing through voluntary insurance for the old age of the worthy poor. He was not quite the first of the philosophers to dream of the abolition of war, and to plan an international tribunal for the settlement of disputes between nations. In that he followed Leibnitz, as he anticipated Kant.

It was such an essentially cold and calculating intellect as this which in that age of ferment could launch the new doctrine of the infinite perfectibility of mankind. Modern readers know the Rev. Dr. Price only from the fulminations of Burke, in whose pages he figures now as an incendiary and again as a fool. He was in point of fact the soul of sobriety and the mirror of all the respectabilities in his serious dissenting world. It is worth while to note that he was also, with his friend Priestley, perhaps the only English Nonconformist preacher who has ever enjoyed a European reputation. No less a man than Condorcet refers to him as one of the formative minds of the century.

12 SHELLEY AND GODWIN

Dr. Price's sermon is worth a glance, not merely because it was the goad which provoked Burke to eloquent fury, but still more because it is a document which records for us the mood in which even the older and graver progressives of his generation greeted the French Revolution. It was an official discourse delivered before the Society for Commemorating the Revolution in Great Britain. This typically English club claimed to have met annually since 1688 for a dinner and a sermon. The centenary of our own Revolution and the events in France gave it for a moment a central place on the political stage. It was an eminently respectable society, mainly composed of middle-class Nonconformists, with four Doctors of Divinity on its Committee, an entrance fee of half-a-guinea, and a radical peer, Earl Stanhope, for its Chairman. At its annual meeting in November, 1789, Dr. Price " disdaining national partialities and rejoicing in every triumph of liberty and justice over arbitrary power," had moved an address congratulating the French National Assembly on " the Revolution in that country and on the prospect it gives to the two first kingdoms in the world of a common participation in the blessings of civil and religious liberty." The

THE FRENCH REVOLUTION 13

sermon was an eloquent expansion of this address.

It opens with a defence of the cosmopolitan attitude which could rejoice at an improvement in the prospects of our hereditary rival. Christ taught not patriotism, but universal benevolence, as the parable of the Good Samaritan shows. "My neighbour" is he to whom I can do most good, whether foreigner or fellow-citizen. We should love our country " ardently but not exclusively," considering ourselves " citizens of the world," and taking care " to maintain a just regard to the rights of other countries." Patriotism had been in history a scourge of mankind. It was among the Romans no better than " a principle holding together a band of robbers in their attempts to crush all liberty but their own." The aim of those who love their kind can be only to spread Truth, Virtue and Liberty. To make mankind happy and free, it should suffice to instruct them. " Ignorance is the parent of bigotry, intolerance, persecution and slavery. Inform and instruct mankind and these evils will be excluded." There follow some rambling remarks on the need for a revisal of the Liturgy and the Articles, a complaint of the servility shown in a recent address to King George, who ought to consider himself rather the servant than the sovereign of his people, and a prediction that France and England, each delivered from despotism by a happy revolution, will now "not merely refrain from engaging in wars with one another, but unite in preventing wars everywhere." As for our own Revolution of 1688, it was a great but not a perfect work. It had left religious toleration incomplete and the Parliamentary franchise unequal. We must continue to enforce its principles, especially in the matter of removing the disabilities that still weigh upon dissenters. Those principles are briefly (1) Liberty of Conscience. (2) The right to resist power when it is abused, and (3) The right to choose our own governors, to cashier them for misconduct and to frame a government for ourselves. There follows a curious little moral exhortation which shows how far the good Dr. Price was from forgetting his duties as a preacher. He had been distressed by the lax morals of some of his colleagues in the agitation for Reform, and he pauses to deplore that "not all who are zealous in this cause are as conspicuous for purity of morals as for ability." He cannot reconcile himself to the idea of an immoral patriot, and begs that they will at least

THE FRENCH REVOLUTION 15

hide their vices. The old man finds his peroration in Simeon's prayer. He had seen the great salvation. "I have lived to see thirty millions of people indignant and resolute, spurning at slavery and demanding liberty with an irresistible voice, their king led in triumph and an arbitrary monarch surrendering himself to his subjects. And now methinks I see the ardour for liberty catching and spreading, a general amendment beginning in human affairs; the dominion of kings changed for the dominion of laws, and the dominion of priests giving way to the dominion of reason and conscience."

The world remembers the scholar Salmasius only because he provoked Milton to a learned outbreak of bad manners. There is something immortal even in the ill-temper of great men, and Dr. Price lives in modern memory chiefly because he moved Burke to declamatory rage. His *Reflections on the French Revolution* was an answer to the Old Jewry sermon, which, eloquent itself, was to beget much eloquence in others. For four years the mighty debate went on, and it became as the disputants conversed across the echoes of the Terror, rather a dialogue between the past and the future, than a discussion between human voices. Burke answered Dr.

SHELLEY AND GODWIN

Price, and to Burke in turn replied Tom Paine with the brilliant, confident, hard-hitting logic of a pamphlet (*The Rights of Man*) which for all the efforts of Pitt to suppress it, is still read and circulated to-day. Two notable answers were ephemeral, one from Mary Wollstonecraft, and another (*Vindiciae Gallicae*) from Mackintosh, who afterwards recanted his own opinions and lived to be known as Sir James.

To lift the discussion to the height of a philosophical argument was reserved for William Godwin, a mind steeped in the French and English speculation of his century, gifted with rare powers of analysis, and inspired with a faith in human reason in general and his own logical capacity in particular, which no English mind before him or after him has approached. In spite of a lucid style and a certain cold eloquence which illumines if it does not warm, Godwin's *Political Justice* was dead before its author, while Burke lives and was never more widely read than to-day.

The ghosts of great men have an erratic habit in walking. It is passion rather than any mere intellectual momentum which drives them from the tomb. There is, moreover, in Burke a variety and a humanity which appeals in some one of its phases and moods to all of us in turn. The great storehouse of his emotions and his phrases has the catholicity of the Bible. Each man can find in it what he seeks. He is like the luminous phantom which walked in *Faust* through the witcheries of the Brocken. Each man saw in her his own first love. He has been hero and prophet to Whigs and Tories, and in our own generation we have seen him bequeath an equal inspiration to a Cecil and a Morley. It is no part of our task to attempt even the briefest exposition of his philosophy; we are concerned with him here chiefly as an influence which helped by its vehemence and its superb rhetorical exaggerations to drive the revolutionary thinkers who answered him to parallel exaggerations and opposite extremes. Inspired himself with a distrust of generalisation, and a hatred of philosophers, he none the less evolved a philosophy as he talked. Against his will he was forced into the upper air in his furious pursuit of the " political aeronauts." His was a volcanic intellect which flung up principles in its moments of eruption, and poured them forth pell-mell with the vituperations and the exaltations.

No logical dissection can reach the inner

truth of Burke. Every statement of a principle in an orator or a pamphleteer is coloured by the occasion, the emotion, and the mood of an audience to whom it is addressed. Burke spoke amid the angers and alarms inspired first by the subversive energy, and then by the doctrinaire cruelty of the French Revolution. It was in the process of " diffusing the Terror " that most of his philosophical *obiter dicta* were uttered. The real nerve of the thinking of a mind so vehement, so passionate, so essentially dramatic is to be sought not in some principle which was the major premise of his syllogisms, but in some pervading emotion. Fanny Burney said of him that when he spoke of the Revolution his face immediately assumed " the expression of a man who is going to defend himself against murderers." That is exactly the tone of all his later utterances. His mission was to spread panic because he felt it. By no other reading can one explain or excuse the rage of his denunciation of the excellent Dr. Price.

If his was philosophy it was philosophy seeing red. He predicted the Terror before it occurred, and by his work in stirring Europe to the coalition against France, he did much to realise his own forebodings.

THE FRENCH REVOLUTION 19

But, to do Burke justice, his was a disinterested fear, and it would be fairer to call it a hatred of cruelty. Burke was not a man to take fire because he thought a principle false. His was rather the practical logic which found a principle false because it led to evil; and the evil which caused his mind to blaze was nearly always cruelty. He hated the French philosophers because in the groves of their Academy " at the end of every vista you see nothing but the gallows." He pursued Rousseau and Dr. Price because their teaching, on his reading of cause and effect, had set the tumbrils rolling and weighted the guillotine for Marie Antoinette. It was precisely the same impulse which had caused him to pursue Warren Hastings for his cruelties towards the Begums of Oude. The spring of all this speculation was a nerve which twitched with a maddening sensitiveness at the sight of suffering.

To rouse Burke's genius to its noblest utterance, there must needs be a suffering which he could personify and dramatise. He saw nothing of the dull peasant misery which in truth explained the Revolution. He ignored those catalogues of injustice and wrong that composed the mandates (the *cahiers*) which the Deputies carried with them to the National

Assembly. He forgot the famines, the exactions, the oppressive privileges which made revolt, and saw only the pathos of the Queen's helplessness before it. In Paine's immortal epigram, he " pitied the plumage and forgot the dying bird." But it is paradoxically true that while he pursued the friends of humanity, his real impulse was the hatred of cruelty which modern men call humanitarian. To that hatred he was always true. No abstract principle, but always this dominating passion, covers his inconsistencies, and bridges the gulf between his earlier Whiggery and his later Toryism. In the French Revolution he saw only cruelty, and he opposed it as he had opposed Indian Imperialism, negro slavery, the savage criminal justice of his day, and the penal laws against the Irish Catholics. Of Burke one must ask not so much What did he believe ? as Whom did he pity ?

It was the contrast of temperament and attitude which made the cleavage between Burke and the friends of the French Revolution deep and irreconcilable. In the fundamentals of political theory he often seems to agree with some of them, and they differ as often among themselves. Burke seems often to retain the typical eighteenth century fiction that the State is based on some original pact or social contract. That was Rousseau's starting point, and it was Godwin's work (after Hume) to shatter this heritage which French and English speculation had been content to accept from Locke. There are passages in which Burke appears to accept the notion, unintelligible to modern minds, of the natural, or as he put it, " primitive," rights of man. He reserved his contempt for those who sought to tabulate or codify these rights, and he would always brush aside any argument based upon them, by asking the prior question, what in the given emergency was best for the good of society, or the happiness of men. Paine, when he was in his more *a priori* moods, was capable of deducing his whole practical system from the abstract rights of man; Godwin was a modern in virtually dismissing the whole notion. While Burke was belabouring Dr. Price, he whittled away the whole theoretic significance of the English Revolution of 1688, but he remained its partisan. He tried to deny Dr. Price's claim to " choose our governors," but he could not relapse into the seventeenth-century Tory doctrine of non-resistance, and would always allow in extreme cases the right of rebellion. Here again there was no final opposition, for there are passages in Godwin against rash rebellion and the anarchy of revolution more impressive, if less emotional, than anything in Burke.

Modern criticism is disposed to base the greatness of Burke on his inspired anticipation of the historical view of politics. Quotation has made classical those noble passages which glorify the continuous life of mankind, link the present by a chain of pieties to the past, conjure up a glowing vision of the social organism, and celebrate the wisdom of our ancestors and the infallibility of the race. There was, indeed, a real opposition of temperament here ; but Burke had no monopoly of the historical vision. It is a travesty to suggest that the revolutionary school despised history. Paine, indeed, was a self-taught man, who knew nothing of history and cared less. But Godwin wrote history with success and even penned a remarkable essay (*On Sepulchres*) in which he anticipated the Comtist veneration for the great dead, and proposed a national scheme for covering the country with monuments to their memory. Condorcet, perhaps the greatest intellect and certainly the noblest character among them, wrote the first attempt at a systematic evolutionary interpretation of history.

But it makes some difference whether a

THE FRENCH REVOLUTION 23

man sees history from above or from below. Burke saw it from the comfortable altitude of the Whig aristocracy to which he had allied himself. The revolutionary school saw its inverse, from the standpoint of the " swinish multitude " (an angry indiscretion of Burke's) for whom it had worked to less advantage. Paine was a man of the people, and Godwin belonged by birth to the dissenting community for whom history had been chiefly a record of persecution, illuminated by rebellion. For Burke the product of history was the sacred constitution in which he saw an " entailed heritage," the social fabric " well cramped and bolted together in all its parts." For Godwin it was mainly a chronicle of criminal wars, savage oppressions, and social misery. Burke, in a moment of paradoxical exaltation, was capable of singing the praises of " prejudice," which " renders a man's virtue his habit." For Condorcet, on the other hand, history was the orderly procession of the human mind, advancing through a series of well-marked epochs (he enumerated nine) from the pastoral state to the French Revolution, each epoch marked primarily by the shedding of some moral, social, or theological " prejudice," which had hampered its advance

It is easy to criticise the naïve intellectualism of such a view as this, which ignores or thrusts into the background the economic causes of advance and retrogression. But it is certainly not an unhistorical view. Burke dreaded fundamental discussions which " turn men's duties into doubts." The revolutionary school believed that all progress depended on the daring and thoroughness of these discussions. History for them was a continuous Socratic dialogue, in which the philosophers of innovation were always arrayed against the sophists of authority. They hoped everything from the leadership of the illuminated few who gradually permeate the mass and raise it with them. Burke held that " the individual is foolish, but the species is wise," and the " natural aristocracy " in whom he trusted was to keep the inert mass in a condition of stable equilibrium.

We retain from Burke to-day the sonorous generalisations, the epigrammatic maxims, which each of us applies in his own way. But to Burke's contemporaries they meant only one thing—a defence of the unreformed franchise. All his reverence for the pre-ordained order of providence, the " divine tactic " which had made society what it was, meant for them in bald prose that Old Sarum should

THE FRENCH REVOLUTION 25

have two members. Burke had not "a doubt that the House of Commons represents perfectly the whole commons of Great Britain." They, with no mystical view of history to guide them, pointed out that its electors were a mere handful of 12,000 in the whole population, and that Birmingham, Manchester, Leeds, Sheffield and Bradford had not a Member among them. While Burke perorated about the ways of providence, they pointed to that auctioneer who put up for sale to the highest bidder the fee simple of the Borough of Gatton with the power of nominating two members for ever. That auctioneer is worth quoting : " Need I tell you, gentlemen, that this elegant contingency is the only infallible source of fortune, titles, and honours in this happy country ? That it leads to the highest situations in the State ? And that, meandering through the tempting sinuosities of ambition, the purchaser will find the margin strewed with roses, and his head quickly crowned with those precious garlands that flourish in full vigour round the fountain of honour ? On this halcyon sea, if any gentleman who has made his fortune in either of the Indies chooses once more to embark, he may repose in perfect quiet. No hurricanes to dread ; no tormenting claims of insolent electors to evade; no tinkers' wives to kiss. . . . With this elegant contingency in his pocket, the honours of the State await his plucking, and with its emoluments his purse will overflow."

A reference to the elegant contingency of Gatton sufficed to deflate a good deal of eloquence.

Burke, indeed, believed in the pre-ordained order of the world, but he somehow omitted the rebels. When in his sublimest periods, he appealed to "the known march of the ordinary providence of God," and saw in revolution and change an assault on the divine order, one sees, rigid and forbidding, the limitations of his thinking. The man who sees in history a divine tactic must salute the regiment in its headlong charge no less than the regiment which stands with fixed bayonets around the ark of the covenant. Said the Hindoo saint, who saw all things in God and God in all things, to the soldier who was slaying him, "And Thou also art He." The march of providence embraced 1789 as well as 1688. Paine and Godwin, Danton and Robespierre might have answered Burke with a reminder that they also were His children.

The key to any understanding of the dialogue between Burke and the Revolutionists

THE FRENCH REVOLUTION 27

is that each side was moved by a passion which meant nothing to the other. Burke was hoarse with anger and fear at the excesses in France. They were afire with an almost religious faith in human perfectibility. Burke's is a great record of detailed reforms achieved or advocated, but for organic change there was no place in his system, and he indulged in no vision of human progress. " The only moral trust with any certainty in our hands," he wrote, " is the care of our own time." It was of to-morrow that the Revolution thought, and even of the day after to-morrow. Nothing could shake its faith. Proscribed amid the Terror for his moderation and independence, learning daily in the garret where he hid of the violent deaths of friends and comrades, witnessing, as it must have seemed to him, the ruin of his work and the frustration of his brightest hopes, Condorcet, solitary and disguised, sat down to write that sketch of human destinies which is, perhaps, the most confident statement of a reasoned optimism in European literature. He finished his *Sketch for an Historical Picture of the Progress of the Human Mind*, left his garret, and went out to meet his death. A year later, as if to show that the great prodigal hope could survive the brain that conceived it, the representatives of the French people had it circulated as a national document.

Its thesis is that no limit can be set to the perfection of human faculties, that the progress and perfectibility of man are independent of any power which can arrest them, and have no term unless it be the duration of the globe itself. The progress might be swift or slow, but the ultimate end was sure. Twenty years before, Turgot projecting a system of universal education in France, had promised to transform the nation in ten years. Condorcet was less sanguine, but his perspective was short. The indefinite advance of mankind presupposed, he argued, the elimination of inequality (1) among peoples, and (2) among classes, and lastly the perfection of the individual. For all this he believed that the Revolution had already laid the foundation. Negro slavery, for example, would end; Africa would enter on a phase of culture dependent on settled agriculture, and the East adopt free institutions. The time was at hand when the sun would rise only on free men, and tyrants, slaves, and priests would live only in history. The Revolution had proclaimed the equality of men, and the future would proceed to realise it. Mono-

THE FRENCH REVOLUTION 29

polies abolished, fortunes would tend to a level of equality, and a system of insurance (Dr. Price's specific) would mitigate or abolish poverty. Universal education would reduce the natural inequality of talents, and break down the barriers of class, so that men, retaining still the desire to be instructed by others, would no longer need to be controlled by their superiors. Science had made a dizzy progress in the past generation, but its advance must be still more rapid when general education enables it to be cultivated by still greater numbers, and by women as well as men. To the fear which Malthus afterwards used as the most formidable argument against revolutionary optimism, that a denser population would leave the means of subsistence inadequate, he opposed intensive cultivation, synthetic chemistry, and the progress of mankind in self-control and virtue. Human character itself will change with the amendment of human institutions. Passion can be dominated by reflection, and by the deliberate encouragement of gentle and altruistic sentiments. The business of politics is to destroy the opposition between self-interest and altruism, and to make a world in which when a man seeks his own good, he need no longer infringe the good of others.

A great share in this moral elevation would come from the destruction of the inequality of the sexes, which Condorcet preached in France while Mary Wollstonecraft was its pioneer in England. That inequality has been ruinous even to the sex which it favoured, and rests in nothing but an abuse of force. To remove it is not merely to raise the status of women but to increase family happiness, and to reform morals. Wars too will end, and with them a constant menace to liberty. The ultimate dream is a perpetual confederation of mankind.

It would be a fascinating but too protracted study to follow this faith in the perfectibility of mankind to its final enthusiasms of prophecy, and to trace it to its origins in the speculations of Helvétius and Holbach, of Priestley and Price. It was a creative impulse which made for itself a psychology and a sociology; it rather led the thinking of men than followed from their reasonings. They seem at every turn to choose of two alternative views the one which would favour this sovereign hope. Is it reason and opinion, or some innate character which governs the actions of men ? The philosophers of hope answer " opinion," for opinion can be indefinitely changed and led from prejudice to

THE FRENCH REVOLUTION

science. Is it climate (as Montesquieu had urged) or political institutions which differentiate the races of men ? Clearly it is institutions, for if it were climate there would be nothing to hope from reform. Burke opposed to all their schemes of construction and destruction, to their generalisations and philosophisings, the unchangeable fact of human nature. They answered (diving into Helvétius) that human nature is itself the product of " education " or, as we should call it, " environment." Circumstances and above all political institutions have made man what he is. Princes, as Holbach puts it, are gardeners who can by varying systems of cultivation alter the character of men as they would alter the form of trees. Change the institutions and you will change human nature itself. There seemed no limit to the improvement which would follow if we could but discard the fetters of prejudice and despotism.

Wordsworth's " shades of the prison-house " which close upon the growing boy, were an echo of this thought. Godwin's friend, Holcroft, embodied it in a striking metaphor : " Men do not become what by nature they are meant to be, but what society makes them. The generous feelings and higher propensities of the soul are, as it were shrunk up, seared, violently wrenched, and amputated, to fit us for our intercourse in the world, something in the manner that beggars maim and mutilate their children to make them fit for their future situation in life."

The men of the Revolution phrased that idea each in his own way, according as they had been influenced, primarily, by Rousseau, Helvétius, or Condorcet. It gave to their controversy with Burke the appearance, not so much of a dispute between rival schools, as of a dialogue between men who spoke to each other in unknown tongues.

* * * * *

Burke condescended to reason with Dr. Price. But the main answer of authority to the friends of the French Revolution, was the answer which Burke prescribed for "infidels"—"a refutation by criminal justice." A curious parallel movement towards extremes went on simultaneously in the two camps. While Burke separated himself from Fox, split the Whig party, and devoted his genius to the task of fanning the general English dislike of the Revolution into a panic rage of anger and fear, the progressive camp in its turn was gradually captured by the "intellectuals," and passed from a humdrum demand for political reform into a ferment of

THE FRENCH REVOLUTION

moral and social speculation. Societies grew up in all the chief centres of population, always with the same programme. "An honest Parliament. An annual Parliament. A Parliament wherein each individual will have his representative." Of these the most active, the most extreme, and the best organised was undoubtedly the London Corresponding Society.

It was founded by a Scottish boot-maker named Thomas Hardy. The sober, limited character of the man is plain to read in his records and pamphlets. The son of a sea-captain, who had had his education in a village school in Perthshire where the scholars paid a penny a week, he was a leading member of the Scots' Kirk in Covent Garden, and had drawn his political education not at all from godless French philosophers, but from the Protestant fanatic, Lord George Gordon, and from Dr. Price's book on the American War. He gathered his own friends together to found his society, and nine of them met for the first time in the "Bell" tavern in Exeter Street in January, 1792. "They had finished their daily labour and met there by appointment. After having their bread and cheese and porter for supper, as usual, and their pipes afterwards, with some conversation, on the hardness of the times and the dearness of all the necessaries of life, which they in common with their fellow-citizens felt to their sorrow, the business for which they had met was brought forward—Parliamentary Reform."

The Corresponding Society drew the bulk of its members from tradesmen, mechanics and shopkeepers, who contributed their penny a week, and organised itself under Hardy's methodical guidance into numerous branches each with twenty members. It is said to have counted in the end some 30,000 members in London alone. It was a focus of discontent and hope which soon attracted men of more conspicuous talents and wider experience. Horne Tooke, man about town, ex-clergyman, and philologist, who had been at first the friend and lieutenant and then the rival and enemy of Wilkes, was there to bridge the years between the last great popular agitation and the new hopes of reform. He was a man cautious and even timid in action, but there was a vanity in him which led him to say " hanging matters " when he had an inflammable audience in front of him within the four walls of a room. There was Tom Paine, the man who had first dared to propose the independence of the United States, a veteran of revolution who had served on Washington's

THE FRENCH REVOLUTION 85

staff, penned those brilliant exhortations which led the American rebels to victory, and acted as Foreign Secretary to the insurgent Congress. On the fringes of the little inner circle of intellectuals one catches a glimpse of William Blake the poet, and Ritson, the first teacher and theorist of vegetarianism. Not the least interesting member of the group was Thomas Holcroft, the inseparable friend and ally of William Godwin. Holcroft's vivid and masterful personality stands out indeed as the most attractive among the abler members of the circle. The son of a boot-maker, he had earned his bread as cobbler, ostler, village schoolmaster, strolling player and reporter. His insatiable passion for knowledge had given him a mastery of French and German. He went in 1783 to Paris as correspondent of the *Morning Herald*, on the modest salary of a guinea-and-a-half a week. It was there that he acquired his familiarity with the writings of the French political philosophers, and performed the quaint achievement of pirating *Figaro* for the English stage. No printed copy was obtainable, and Holcroft contrived to commit the whole play to memory by attending ten performances, much as Mozart had pirated the ancient exclusive music of St. Peter's in Rome. He was at this period a thriving literary craftsman, and the author of a series of popular plays in which the critics of the time had just begun to note and resent an obtrusive democratic tendency.

Under the influence of these eager speculative spirits, the Corresponding Society must have travelled far from its original business of Parliamentary Reform. Here is an extract from evidence given before the Privy Council, which relates the proceedings at one of its later meetings:

" The most gentlemanlike person took the chair and talked about an equal representation of the people, and of putting an end to war. Holcroft talked about the Powers of the Human Mind. . . . Mr. Holcroft talked a great deal about Peace, of his being against any violent or coercive means, that were usually resorted to against our fellow-creatures, urged the more powerful operation of Philosophy and Reason to convince man of his errors; that he would disarm his greatest enemy by these means and oppose his Fury. He spoke also about Truth being powerful, and gave advice to the above effect to the delegates present who all seemed to agree, as no person opposed his arguments."

One may doubt, however, whether the whole

society was composed of " natural Quakers," who, like Holcroft and Godwin, preached non-resistance before Tolstoy. The dour commonsense of Hardy maintained the theory —he vowed that it was only theory—that every citizen should possess arms and know their use. As the Revolution went forward in France, the agitation in England became increasingly reckless. When the society held its anniversary dinner after the Terror, in May, 1794, at the " Crown and Anchor " Tavern, the band played " Ça ira," the " Carmagnole " and the " Marseillaise." The chief toasts were " the Rights of Man," and " the Armies contending for Liberty," which was a sufficiently clear phrase for describing the Republican armies that were at war with England. There followed an ode composed by Sir William Jones, a translation of the Athenian song which celebrated the deeds of the tyrannicides, Harmodius and Aristogeiton ;

> Verdant myrtle's branchy pride
> Shall my thirsty blade entwine.

One may doubt whether Sir William Jones ever felt the smallest inclination to satisfy the thirst of his blade, but there was provision enough for more commonplace appetites. Two years before, Hardy's worthy mechanics had supped on porter and cheese and talked of the hardness of the times. Their movement had been captured by a group of eager, sophisticated, literary persons, who went much farther than Parliamentary Reform, and with the aid of claret and the subtler French intoxicants, "turned indignant" as another Ode puts it:

> From Kings who seek in Gothic night
> To hide the blaze of moral light.
> Fill high the animating glass
> And let the electric ruby pass.

It was a cheerful indignation, a festive rage.

That dinner must have marked the height of the revolutionary tide in England. The reaction was already rampant and vindictive, and before the year 1794 was out it had crushed the progressive movement and postponed for thirty-eight years the triumph of Parliamentary Reform. It requires a strenuous exercise of the imagination to conceive the panic which swept over England as the news of the French Terror circulated. It fastened impartially on every class of the community, and destroyed the emotional balance no less of Pitt and his colleagues than of the working men who formed the Church and King mobs. Proclamations were issued to

THE FRENCH REVOLUTION

quell insurrections which never had been planned, and the militia called out when not a hand had been raised against the King throughout Great Britain. So great was the fear, so deep the moral indignation that " even respectable and honest men," (the phrase is Holcroft's) " turned spies and informers on their friends from a sense of public duty." A mob burned Dr. Priestley's house near Birmingham for no better reason than because he was supposed to have attended a Reform dinner, which in fact, he did not attend. Hardy's bookshop in Piccadilly was rushed by a mob, and his wife, about to be confined, was injured in her efforts to escape, and died a few hours afterwards. A hunt went on all over the kingdom for booksellers and printers to prosecute, and when Thomas Paine was prosecuted in his absence for publishing *The Rights of Man*, the jury was so determined to find him guilty that they would not trouble to hear the case for the Crown.

Twenty years before, the French philosopher Helvétius, after an experience of Jesuit persecution and Court disfavour in France, made a quaint proposal for re-organising the whole discussion of moral and political questions. The first step, he thought, was to compile a dictionary in which all the terms required in such debates would receive an authoritative definition. But this dictionary, he urged, must be composed in the English language, and published first in England, for only there was discussion free, and the press unfettered. In the reaction over which Pitt and Dundas presided, that envied liberty was totally eclipsed. The *Habeas Corpus* Act was suspended; the Privy Council sat as a sort of Star Chamber to question political suspects, and there was even talk of importing Hessian and Hanoverian mercenaries to check an insurrection which nowhere showed its head. The frailest of all human endowments is the sense of humour. The sense of proportion had been eclipsed in the panic, and most of the cases which may be studied to-day in the State trials impress the modern reader as tasteless and cruel farces. Men were tried and sentenced never for deeds, but always for words. For a sermon closely resembling Dr. Price's, a dissenting minister named Winterbotham was tried at Exeter, and sentenced to four years' imprisonment and a fine of £200. The attorney, John Frost, returning from France, admitted in a chance conversation in a coffee-house that he thought society could manage very well without kings; he was

THE FRENCH REVOLUTION 41

imprisoned, set in the pillory and struck off the rolls. One favourite expedient was to produce a spy who would swear that he had heard some suspect Radical declare in a coach or a coffee-house, that he would "as soon have the King's head off as he would tear a bit of paper" (evidence against a group of Manchester prisoners), or that he "would cut off the King's head as easily as he would shave himself" (case against Thomas Hardy). The climax of really entertaining absurdity was reached when two debtors imprisoned in the Fleet were tried and sentenced for nailing a seditious libel to its doors. The libel was a notice that "This house is to let," that "infamous bastilles are no longer necessary in Europe," and that "peaceable possession" would be secured "on or before the first day of January, 1793, being the commencement of the first year of liberty in Great Britain."

The farce of this panic became a tragedy when the reformers of Scotland ventured to summon a Convention at Edinburgh to voice the demand for shorter Parliaments and universal male suffrage. It met in October, 1793, and was attended by delegates from the London Corresponding Society as well as from Scottish branches. Nothing was intended beyond the holding of what we should call to-day a conference or congress. But the word "Convention" with its reminiscence of the French revolutionary assembly seems to have caused the Government some particular alarm. The Convention, after some days of orderly debate, was invaded by the magistrates and broken up. Margarot and Sinclair (the English delegates), Skirving, Palmer and Thomas Muir, were tried before that notorious hanging judge, whom Stevenson portrayed as Weir of Hermiston, and sentenced to fourteen years' deportation at Botany Bay.

Of these five, all of them young men of brilliant promise and high courage, only one, Margarot, lived to return to England. Muir, daring, romantic and headstrong, contributed to the history of the movement a page of adventure which might invite the attention of a novelist. He escaped from Botany Bay on a whaler, was wrecked on the coast of South America, contrived to wander to the West Indies, there shipped on a Spanish vessel for Europe, fell in with an English frigate, was wounded in the fight that followed, and had the good fortune to find among the officers who took him prisoner an old friend, who recognised him, and assisted him to conceal his identity. He was landed in

THE FRENCH REVOLUTION 43

Spain, invited to Paris and pensioned by the Convention, but died shortly after his arrival. Less romantic but even finer is Sinclair's story. He obtained bail while his comrades were tried and sentenced. He might have broken his bail, and his friends urged him to do so, but with the certainty that Botany Bay lay before him he none the less returned to Edinburgh, as Horne Tooke puts it " in discharge of his faith as a private man towards his bail, and in discharge of his duty towards an oppressed and insulted public; he has returned not to take a fair trial, but, as he is well persuaded, to a settled conviction and sentence." Joseph Gerrald, another member of the same group gave the same fine example of courage, surrendered to his bail, and was sent for fifteen years to Botany Bay.

The ferment was more than an intellectual stirring. It brought with it a moral elevation and a great courage that did not shrink from venturing life and fortune for a disinterested end. The modern reader is apt to indulge a smile when he reads in the ardent declamation of this time professions of a love of Virtue and praises of Universal Benevolence. We are impatient of abstractions and shy of capital letters. But it was no abstraction which carried a man with honour to the fevers and privations of Botany Bay, when he might have sought safety and fame in Paris. The English reformers were resolved to brave the worst that Pitt could do to them, and challenged the fate of their Scottish comrades. They prepared in their turn to hold a "Convention" for Parliamentary Reform, and showed a doubtful prudence in keeping its details secret while the intention was boldly avowed. The counter-stroke came promptly. Twelve of the leading members of the Corresponding Society, including Hardy, Horne Tooke and Holcroft were arrested and sent, for the most part to the Tower, on a charge of high treason. The records of their preliminary examination before the Privy Council go to show that Pitt and Dundas had allowed themselves to be persuaded by their spies that every species of treason and folly was in preparation, from an armed insurrection down to a plan to murder the King by blowing a poisoned arrow from an air-gun. The Government had said that there was a treasonable conspiracy; it had to produce the traitors.

There was some delay in arresting Holcroft. His conduct is worth recording because it is so typical of the naïve courage, the doctrinaire hardihood of the group. These men whom the reaction accused of subverting morality, were in fact dervishes of principle, who rushed on the bayonets in the name of manhood and truth and sincerity. Godwin when he came in his systematic treatise to describe how a free people would conduct a defensive war, declared that it would scorn to resort to a stratagem or an ambuscade. In the same spirit Holcroft hearing that a warrant was out against him for high treason, walked boldly into the Chief Justice's court, and announced that he came to be put upon his trial "that if I am a guilty man, the whole extent of my guilt may become notorious, and if innocent that the rectitude of my principles and conduct may be no less public." When a messenger did, in fact, go to Holcroft's house about the same hour to arrest him, his daughters, obedient to the same ideal of sincerity, actually invited him to take their father's papers.

One may doubt whether English liberties have ever run a graver danger in modern times than at the trial of the twelve reformers. The Government sought to overwhelm them with a mass of evidence which they lacked the means to sift and confute. But no definite act was charged against them, and the whole case turned on a monstrous attempt to give a wide constructive interpretation to the law of high treason. High treason in English law has the perfectly definite meaning of an attempt on the King's life, or the levying of war against him. Chief Justice Eyre, in his charge to the Grand Jury, sought to stretch it until it assumed a Russian latitude, and would include any effort by agitation to alter the form of government or the constitution of Parliament. The issue, before a jury which probably had not escaped the general panic, seemed very doubtful, and it was the general opinion that the decisive blow for liberty was struck by William Godwin. Long years afterwards Horne Tooke, in a dramatic scene, called Godwin to him in public, and kissed the hand which had saved his life.

Godwin contributed to the *Morning Chronicle* a long letter, or more properly, a pamphlet, in which he analysed the Chief Justice's charge and brought to the light what really was latent in it, a claim to treat as high treason any effort, however peaceful and orderly, to bring about a fundamental change in our institutions. The letter shows none of Godwin's speculative daring, and his gift of cold and dignified eloquence is severely repressed. He wrote to attain his immediate end, and from that standpoint his pleading was a masterpiece.

THE FRENCH REVOLUTION

A certain deadly courtesy, a tone of quiet reasonableness made it possible for the most prejudiced reader to follow it with assent. The argument was irresistible, and the single touch of emotion at the end was worthy of a great orator. A few lines depicted these men who, moved by public spirit, had acted in good faith within the law, as it had been universally understood in England, overwhelmed by a sudden extension of its most terrible articles, applied to them without precedent or warning. Should the awful sentence be read over these men, that they should be hanged (but not until they were dead), and then, still living, suffer the loss of their members and see their bowels torn out? The ghastly barbarity of the whole procedure could not have been more effectively exposed. Looking back upon this trial there is no reason to think that the reformers exaggerated its importance. Had the Government won its case, it must have succeeded in destroying the very possibility of opposition or agitation in England. It was believed that no less than three hundred signed warrants lay ready for issue on the day that Hardy and his friends were convicted. But the stroke was too daring, the threat too impudent. When the trial began, the prosecution lightened its own task by dropping the charge against Holcroft and three of his comrades. But for nine days the charge was pressed against Thomas Hardy, and when he was acquitted a further six days was spent in the effort to convict Horne Tooke, and four in a last vain attempt to succeed against Thelwall.

The popular victory checked the excesses of the reaction. As Holcroft wrote: " The whole power of Government was directed against Thomas Hardy: in his fate seemed involved the fate of the nation, and the verdict of Not Guilty appeared to burst its bonds, and to have released it from inconceivable miseries and ages of impending slavery." The reaction, indeed, was restrained; but so also was the movement of reform. The subsequent history of its leaders is one of unheroic failure, and of an unpopularity which was harder to endure than danger. Windham referred to the twelve in debate as " acquitted felons," and Holcroft was constrained first to produce his plays under a borrowed name, and then to seek a refuge in voluntary exile on the continent. The passions roused by the Terror arrested the progress of the revolutionary movement in England. The alarms and glories of the struggle with Napoleon buried it in oblivion.

THE FRENCH REVOLUTION

It is this complex experience which lies behind Godwin's political writings. The French Revolution produced its simple effects in Burke and Tom Paine—revolt and disgust in the one, enthusiasm and hope in the other. In Godwin the reaction is more complicated. He retained to the last his ardent faith in progress, and the perfectibility of mankind. No events could shake that, but it was the work of experience to reinforce all the native individualism of his confident and self-reliant temper, to harden into an extreme dogma that general belief in *laissez faire* which was the common property of most of the English progressives of his day, and to beget in him not merely a doubt in the efficacy of violent revolutions, but a dislike of all concerted political effort and the whole collective work of political associations. He had felt the lash of repression, saved one friend from the hangman, and seen others depart for Botany Bay: he remained to the end, the uncompromising foe of every species of governmental coercion. He had listened to Horne Tooke perorating "hanging matters" at the Corresponding Society; he had seen the "electric ruby" circulating at its dinners; he had witnessed the collapse of Thomas Hardy's painstaking and methodical organisation. The fruit of all these experiences was the first statement in European literature of philosophic anarchism —a statement which hardly yields to Tolstoy's in its trenchant and unflinching logic.

"Logic" is more often a habit of consecutive and reasoned writing than the source of a thinker's opinion. The logical writer is the man who can succeed in displaying plausible reasons for what he believes by instinct, or knows by experience. There is history and temperament behind the coldest logic. The history which set Godwin against all State action, whether undertaken in defence of order or privilege, or on behalf of reform, is to be read in the excesses of Pitt and the futilities of the Corresponding Society. The question of temperament involves a subtler psychological judgment. If you feel in yourself something less than the heroic temper which will make a militant agitation or a violent revolution against the monstrous ascendency of privilege and ordered force, you are lucky if you can convince yourself that agitation is commonly mischievous, and association but a means of combating one evil by creating another. Godwin was certainly no coward. But he was fortunate in evolving a theory which excused him from attempting the more dangerous exploits of civic courage. His ideal was the Stoic virtue, the isolated strength, which can stand firm in passive protest against oppression and wrong. He stood firm, and Pitt was content to leave him standing.

* * * * *

We have seen the first bold statement of the hope which the French Revolution kindled in Dr. Price's Old Jewry sermon. We have watched the brave incautious effort to realise it in the plans of the Corresponding Society. In these crowded years that began with the fall of the Bastille and closed with the Terror, it was to enter on yet another phase, and in this last incarnation the hope was very near despair. To men in the early prime of life, aware of their powers and their gift of influence, the Revolution came as a call to action. To a group of still younger men, poets and thinkers, forming their first eager views of life in the leisure of the Universities, it was above all a stimulus to fancy. Godwin was their prophet, but they built upon his speculations the superstructure of a dream that was all their own. For some years, Coleridge, Southey, and Wordsworth were caught and held in the close web of logic which Godwin gave to the world in 1793 in the first edition of *Political Justice*. Wordsworth read and studied and continually discussed it. Southey confessed that he "read and studied and all but worshipped Godwin." Coleridge wrote a sonnet which he afterwards suppressed in which he blesses his "holy guidance" and hymns Godwin "with an ardent lay."

> For that thy voice in passion's stormy day
> When wild I roamed the bleak heath of distress
> Bade the bright form of Justice meet my way,
> And told me that her name was Happiness.

To us who read Godwin with many a later Utopia in our memories, his most valuable chapters are those which give his penetrating criticisms of existing society. To these young men the excitement was in his picture of a free community from which laws and coercion had been eliminated, and in which property was in a continual flux actuated by the stream of universal benevolence. They resolved to found a community based on Godwinian principles, and to free themselves from the cramping and dwarfing influences of a society ruined by laws and superstitions, they lit on the simple expedient of removing themselves beyond its reach. They lacked the manhood and the simplicity which had turned more prosaic natures into agitators and reformers. It is a tale which every student of literature

THE FRENCH REVOLUTION 53

has delighted to read, how Coleridge and Southey, bent on founding their Pantisocracy, on the banks of the Susquehana, came to Bristol to charter a ship, and while they waited, dimly aware that they lacked funds for the adventure, anchored themselves in English homes by marrying the Fricker sisters.

As one of the comrades, Robert Lovell, quaintly puts it in a letter to Holcroft, "Principle, not plan, is our object." Lovell had visited Holcroft in gaol, and one can well understand how that near view of the fate which awaited the reformer under Pitt, confirmed them in their idea of crossing the Atlantic. "From the writings of William Godwin and yourself," Lovell went on, "our minds have been illuminated; we wish our actions to be guided by the same superior abilities." Holcroft, older and more combative than his poet-disciples, advised the founding of a model colony in this country. But the lure of a distant scene was too attractive. Cottle, the friend and publisher of the Pantisocrats, has left his account of their aims. Theirs was to be "a social colony in which there was to be a community of property and where all that was selfish was to be proscribed." It would realise "a state of society free from the evils and turmoils that then agitated the world, and present an example of the eminence to which men might arrive under the unrestrained influence of sound principles." It would " regenerate the whole complexion of society, and that not by establishing formal laws, but by excluding all the little deteriorating passions, injustice, wrath, anger, clamor, and evil speaking, and thereby setting an example of human perfectibility."

What is left of the dream to-day? Some verses in Coleridge's earlier poems, the address to Chatterton for instance

> O Chatterton! that thou wert yet alive,
> Sure thou wouldst spread the canvas to the gale;
> And love with us the tinkling team to drive
> O'er peaceful Freedom's undivided dale.

and those lines, half comical, half pathetic, in which the " sweet harper " is assured as some requital for a hard life and a cruel death, that the Pantisocrats will raise a "solemn cenotaph" to his memory "Where Susquehana pours his untamed stream." Long afterwards, Coleridge described Pantisocracy in *The Friend* as " a plan as harmless as it was extravagant," which had served a purpose by saving him from more dangerous courses. " It was serviceable in securing

THE FRENCH REVOLUTION 55

myself and perhaps some others from the paths of sedition. We were kept free from the stains and impurities which might have remained upon us had we been travelling with the crowd of less imaginative malcontents through the dark lanes and foul by-roads of ordinary fanaticism."

Pantisocracy was indeed a happy episode for English literature. One may doubt whether the " Ancient Mariner " would have been written, had Coleridge travelled with Gerrald and Sinclair along the " dark lane " that led to Botany Bay. Nature can work strange miracles with the instinct of self-preservation, and even for poets she has a care. The prudence which teaches one man to be a Whig, will make of another a Utopian.

CHAPTER II

THOMAS PAINE

"Where Liberty is, there is my country." The sentiment has a Latin ring; one can imagine an early Stoic as its author. It was spoken by Benjamin Franklin, and no saying better expresses the spirit of eighteenth century humanity. "Where is not Liberty, there is mine." The answer is Thomas Paine's. It is the watchword of the knight errant, the marching music that sent Lafayette to America, and Byron to Greece, the motto of every man who prizes striving above enjoyment, honours comradeship above patriotism, and follows an idea that no frontier can arrest. Paine was indeed of no century, and no formula of classification can confine him. His writing is of the age of enlightenment; his actions belong to romance. His clear, manly style, his sturdy commonsense, the rapier play of his epigrams, the formal, logical architecture of his thoughts, his complacent limitations, his horror of mystery

THOMAS PAINE

and Gothic half-lights, his harsh contempt for all the sacred muddle of priestly traditions and aristocratic politics, his assurance, his intellectual courage, his humanity—all that, in its best and its worst, belongs to the century of Voltaire and the Revolution. In his spirit of adventure, in his passion for movement and combat, there Paine is romantic. Paine thought in prose and acted epics. He drew horizons on paper and pursued the infinite in deeds.

Tom Paine was born, the son of a Quaker stay-maker, in 1737, at Thetford, in the county of Norfolk. His parents were poor, but he owed much, he tells us, to a good moral education and picked up " a tolerable stock of useful learning," though he knew no language but his own. A " Friend " he was to the end in his independence, his rationalism, and his humanity, though he laughed when he thought of what a sad-coloured world the Quakers would have made of the creation, if they had been consulted. The boy craved adventure, and was prevented at seventeen from enlisting in the crew of the privateer *Terrible*, Captain Death, only to sail somewhat later in the *King of Prussia*, Captain Mendez. One cruise under a licensed pirate was enough for him, and he soon settled in London, making stays for a living and spending his leisure in the study of astronomy. He qualified as an exciseman, acquiring in this employment a grasp of finance and an interest in budgets of which he afterwards made good use in his writings. Cashiered for negligence, he turned schoolmaster, and even aspired to ordination in the Church of England. Reinstated as a " gauger," he was eventually dismissed for writing a pamphlet in defence of the excisemen's agitation for higher wages. He was twice married, but his first wife died within a year of marriage, and the second, with whom he had started a " tobacco-mill," agreed on its failure, apparently for no definite fault on either side, to a mutual separation. At thirty-seven, penniless, lonely, and stamped with failure, yet conscious of powers which had found no scope in the Old World, he emigrated in 1774 to America with a letter from Benjamin Franklin as his passport to fortune.

Opportunity came promptly, and Paine was presently settled in Philadelphia as the editor of the *Pennsylvania Magazine*. From the pages of this periodical, his admirable biographer, Mr. Moncure D. Conway, has unearthed a series of articles which show that Paine had somehow brought with him

THOMAS PAINE

from England a mental equipment which ranked him already among the moral pioneers of his generation. He advocates international arbitration; he attacks duelling; he suggests more rational ideas of marriage and divorce; he pleads for mercy to animals; he demands justice for women. Above all, he assails negro slavery, and with such mastery and fervour, that five weeks after the appearance of his article, the first American Anti-Slavery Society was founded at Philadelphia. The abolition of slavery was a cause for which he never ceased to struggle, and when in later life he became the target of religious persecutors, it was in their dual capacity of Christians and slave-owners that men stoned him. The American colonies were now at the parting of the ways in the struggle with the Mother Country. The revolt had begun with a limited object, and few if any of its leaders realised whither they were tending. Paine it was, who after the slaughter at Lexington, abandoned all thoughts of reconciliation and was the first to preach independence and republicanism.

His pamphlet, *Common-Sense* (1776), achieved a circulation which was an event in the history of printing, and fixed in men's minds as firm resolves what were, before he wrote, no more than fluid ideas. It spoke to rebels and made a nation. Poor though Paine was, he poured the whole of the immense profits which he received from the sale of his little book into the colonial war-chest, shouldered a musket, joined Washington's army as a private, and was soon promoted to be aide-de-camp to General Greene. Paine's most valuable weapon, however, was still his pen. Writing at night, after endless marches, by the light of camp fires at a moment of general depression, when even Washington thought that the game was " pretty well up," Paine began to write the series of pamphlets afterwards collected under the title of *The American Crisis*. They did for the American volunteers what Rouget de Lisle's immortal song did for the French levies in the revolutionary wars, what Körner's martial ballads did for the German patriots in the Napoleonic wars. These superb pages of exhortation were read in every camp to the disheartened men; their courage commanded victory. Burke himself wrote nothing finer than the opening sentences of the first " crisis," a trumpet call indeed, but phrased by an artist who knew the science of compelling music from brass :—

" These are the times that try men's souls. The summer soldier and the sunshine patriot

THOMAS PAINE

will, in this crisis, shrink from the service of his country; but he that stands it now, deserves the thanks of man and woman. Tyranny, like Hell, is not easily conquered; yet we have this consolation with us, that the harder the conflict the more glorious the triumph. What we obtain too cheap we esteem too lightly; it is dearness only that gives everything its value. Heaven knows how to put a proper price upon its goods; and it would be strange indeed if so celestial an article as freedom should not be highly rated."

" Common-sense " Paine was now the chief of the moral forces behind the fighting Republic, and his power of thinking boldly and stating clearly drove it forward to its destiny under the leadership of men whom Nature had gifted with less trenchant minds. He was in succession Foreign Secretary to Congress and clerk to the Pennsylvania Assembly, and we find him converting despair into triumph by the magic of self-sacrifice. He it was who in 1780 saved the finances of the war in a moment of despair, by starting the patriotic subscription with the gift of his own salary, and in 1781 proved his diplomatic gift in a journey to Paris by obtaining money-aid from the French Court.

Paine might have settled down to enjoy his fame, after the war, on the little property which the State of New York gave him. He loathed inaction and escaped middle age. In 1787 he returned to England, partly to carry his pen where the work of liberation called for it, partly to forward his mechanical inventions. Paine, self-educated though he was, was a capable mathematician, and he followed the progress of the applied sciences with passion. His inventions include a long list of things partly useful, partly whimsical, a planing machine, a crane, a smokeless candle and a gunpowder motor. But his fame as an inventor rests on his construction of the first iron bridge, made after his models and plans at Wearmouth. He was received as a leader and teacher in the ardent circle of reformers grouped round the Revolution Society and the Corresponding Society. Others were the dreamers and theorists of liberty. He had been at the making of a Republic, and his American experience gave the stimulus to English Radicalism which events in France were presently to repeat. His fame was already European, and at the fall of the Bastille, it was to Paine that Lafayette confided its key, when a free France sent that symbol of defeated despotism as a present

THOMAS PAINE

to a free America. He seemed the natural link between three revolutions, the one which had succeeded in the New World, the other which was transforming France, and the third which was yet to come in England.

Burke's *Reflections* rang in his ears like a challenge, and he sat promptly down in his inn to write his reply. *The Rights of Man* is an answer to Burke, but it is much more. The vivid pages of history in which he explains and defends the French Revolution which Burke had attacked and misunderstood, are only an illustration to his main argument. He expounds the right of revolution, and blows away the cobweb argument of legality by which his antagonist had sought to confine posterity within the settlement of 1688. Every age and generation must be free to act for itself. Man has no property in man, and the claim of one generation to govern beyond the grave is of all tyrannies the most insolent. Burke had contended for the right of the dead to govern the living, but that which a whole nation chooses to do, it has a right to do. The men of 1688, who surrendered their own rights and bound themselves to obey King William and his heirs, might indeed choose to be slaves; but that could not lessen the right of their children to be free. Wrongs cannot have a legal descent. Here was a bold and triumphant answer to a sophistical argument; but it served Paine only as a preface to his exposition of the American constitution, which was " to Liberty what a grammar is to language," and to his plea for the adoption in England of the French charter of the Rights of Man.

Paine felt that he had made one Republic with a pamphlet, why not another? He had the unlimited faith of his generation in the efficacy of argument, and experience had proved his power. As Carlyle, in his whimsical dramatic fashion, said of him, " He can and will free all this world; perhaps even the other." Godwin, as became the philosopher of the movement, set his hopes on the slower working of education: to make men wise was to make them free. Paine was the pamphleteer of the human camp. He saw mankind as an embattled legion and believed, true man of action that he was, that freedom could be won like victory by the impetus of a resolute charge. He quotes the epigram of his fellow-soldier, Lafayette, " For a nation to love liberty, it is sufficient that she knows it; and to be free it is sufficient that she wills it." Godwin would have sent men to school to liberty; Paine called them to her unfurled

THOMAS PAINE

standard. It is easy to understand the success of Paine's book, which appeared in March, 1791. It was theory and practice in one; it was the armed logic which had driven King George's regiments from America, the edged argument which had razed the Bastille. It was bold reasoning, and it was also inspired writing. Holcroft and Godwin helped to bring out *The Rights of Man*, threatened with suppression or mutilation by the publishers, and a panting incoherent shout of joy in a note from Holcroft to Godwin is typical of the excitement which it caused:—

" I have got it—if this do not cure my cough it is a damned perverse mule of a cough. The pamphlet—from the row—But m_m—we don't sell it—oh, no—ears and eggs—verbatim, except the addition of a short preface, which as you have not seen, I send you my copy.—Not a single castration (Laud be unto God and J. S. Jordan!) can I discover —Hey, for the new Jerusalem! The Millennium! And peace and eternal beatitude be unto the soul of Thomas Paine."

The usual prosecutions of booksellers followed; but everywhere the new societies of reform were circulating the book, and if it helped to send some good men to Botany Bay, copies enough were sold to earn a sum of a thousand pounds for the author, which, with his usual disinterestedness, he promptly gave to the Corresponding Society. A second part appeared in 1792; and at length Pitt adopted Burke's opinion that criminal justice was the proper argument with which to refute Tom Paine. Acting on a hint from William Blake, who, in a vision more prosaic and veridical than was usual with him, had seen the constables searching for his friend, Paine escaped to France, and was convicted in his absence of high treason.

Paine landed at Calais an outlaw, to find himself already elected its deputy to the Convention. As in America, so in France, his was the first voice to urge the uncompromising solution. He advocated the abolition of the monarchy; but his was a courage that always served humanity. The work which he did as a member, with Sieyès, Danton, Condorcet, and five others, of the little committee named to draft the constitution, was ephemeral. His brave pleading for the King's life was a deed that deserves to live. He loved to think of himself as a woodman swinging an axe against rotten institutions and dying beliefs; but he weighted no guillotines. Paine argued against the command that we should " love our enemies," but he would not persecute them. This knight-errant would fling his shield over the very spies who tracked his steps. In Paris he saved the life of one of Pitt's agents who had vilified him, and procured the liberation of a bullying English officer who had struck him in public. The Terror made mercy a traitor, and Paine found himself overwhelmed in the vengeance which overtook all that was noblest in the Revolution. He spent ten months in prison, racked with fever, and an anecdote which seems to be authentic, tells how he escaped death by the negligence of a jailor. This overworked official hastily chalked the sign which meant that a prisoner was marked for next batch of the guillotine's victims, on the inside instead of the outside of Paine's cell-door.

Condorcet, in hiding and awaiting death, wrote in these months his *Sketch* of human progress. Paine, meditating on the end that seemed near, composed the first part of his *Age of Reason*. Paine was, like Franklin, Jefferson and Washington, a deist; and he differed from them only in the courage which prompted him to declare his belief. He came from gaol a broken man, hardly able to stand, while the Convention, returned to its sound senses, welcomed him back to his place of honour on its benches. The record of his last years in America, whither he returned in 1802, belongs rather to the history of persecution than to the biography of a soldier of liberty. His work was done; and, though his pen was still active and influential, slave-owners, ex-royalists, and the fanatics of orthodoxy combined to embitter the end of the man who had dared to deny the inspiration of the Bible. His book was burned in England by the hangman. Bishops in their answers mingled grudging concessions with personal abuse. An agent of Pitt's was hired to write a scurrilous biography of the Government's most dreaded foe. In America, the grandsons of the Puritan colonists who had flogged Quaker women as witches, denied him a place on the stage-coach, lest an offended God should strike it with lightning.

Paine died, a lonely old man, in 1809. His personal character stands written in his career; and it is unnecessary to-day even to mention the libels which his biographer has finally refuted. In a generation of brave men he was the boldest. He could rouse the passions of men, and he could brave them. If the Royalist Burke was eloquent for a Queen, Republican Paine risked his life for a King. No wrong found him indifferent; and he used his pen not only for the democracy which might reward him, but for animals, slaves and women. Poverty never left him, yet he made fortunes with his pen, and gave them to the cause he served. A naïve vanity was his only fault as a man. It was his fate to escape the gallows in England and the guillotine in France. He deserved them both; in that age there was no higher praise. A better democrat never wore the armour of the knight-errant; a better Christian never assailed Orthodoxy.

Neither by training nor by temperament was Paine a speculative thinker; but his political writing has none the less an immense significance. Godwin was a writer removed by his profoundly individual genius from the average thought of his day. Paine agreed more nearly with the advanced minds of his generation, and he taught the rest to agree with him. No one since him or before him has stated the plain democratic case against monarchy and aristocracy with half his spirit and force. Earlier writers on these themes were timid; the moderns are bored. Paine is writing of what he understands, and feels to be of the first importance. He cares as much about abolishing titles as a modern reformer may feel about nationalising land. His main theory in politics has a lucid simplicity. Men are born as God created them, free and equal; that is the assumption alike of natural and revealed religion. Burke, who " fears God," looks with " awe to kings," with " duty to magistrates," and with " respect to nobility," is but erecting a wilderness of turnpike gates between man and his Maker. Natural rights inhere in man by reason of his existence; civil rights are founded in natural rights and are designed to secure and guarantee them. He gives an individual twist to the doctrine of the social compact. Some governments arise out of the people, others over the people. The latter are based on conquest or priestcraft, and the former on reason. Government will be firmly based on the social compact only when nations deliberately sit down as the Americans have done, and the French are doing, to frame a constitution on the basis of the Rights of Man.

As for the English Government, it clearly arose in conquest; and to speak of a British Constitution is playing with words. Parliament, imperfectly and capriciously elected, is supposed to hold the common purse in trust; but the men who vote the supplies are also those who receive them. The national purse is the common hack on which each party mounts in turn, in the countryman's fashion of " ride and tie." They order these things better in France. As for our system of conducting wars, it is all done over the heads of the people. War is with us the art of conquering at home. Taxes are not raised to carry on wars, but wars raised to carry on taxes. The shrewd hard-hitting blows range over the whole surface of existing institutions. Godwin from his intellectual eminence saw in all the follies and crimes of mankind nothing worse than the effects of " prejudice " and the consequences of fallacious reasoning. Paine saw more self-interest in the world than prejudice. When he came to preach the abolition of war, first through an alliance of Britain, America and France, and then through " a confederation of nations " and a European Congress, he saw the obstacle in the egoism of courts and courtiers which appear to quarrel but agree to plunder. Another seven years, he wrote in 1792, would see the end of monarchy and aristocracy in Europe. While they continue, with war as their trade, peace has not the security of a day.

Paine's writing gains rather than loses in

theoretic interest, because the warmth of his sympathies melts, as he proceeds, the icy logic of his eighteenth century individualism. He starts where all his school started, with a sharp antithesis between society and government.

"Society is produced by our wants and government by our wickedness; the former promotes our happiness positively by uniting our affections; the latter negatively by restraining our vices. The one encourages intercourse, the other creates distinctions. The first is a patron, the last a punisher. Society in every state is a blessing; but government even in its best state is a necessary evil. . . . Government, like dress, is the badge of our lost innocence; the palaces of kings are built on the ruins of the bowers of paradise."

That was the familiar pessimism which led in practical politics to *laissez faire*, and in speculation to Godwin's philosophic anarchism. Paine himself seems for a moment to take that road. He enjoys telling us how well the American colonies managed in the early stages of the war without any regular form of government. He assures us that "the more perfect civilisation is, the less occasion has it for government." But he had served an apprenticeship to life; looking

THOMAS PAINE

around him at the streets filled with beggars and the jails crowded with poor men, he suddenly forgets that the whole purpose of government is to secure the individual against the invasion of his rights, and straightway bursts into a new definition :—" Civil government does not consist in executions; but in making such provision for the instruction of youth and the support of age as to exclude as much as possible profligacy from the one and despair from the other. Instead of this the resources of a country are lavished upon kings . . . and the poor themselves are compelled to support the fraud that oppresses them."

It is amazing how much good Paine can extract from a necessary evil. He has suddenly conceived of government as the instrument of the social conscience. He means to use it as a means of securing a better organisation of society. Paine was a man of action, and no mere logic could hold him. He proceeds in a breathless chapter to evolve a programme of social reform which, after the slumbers of a century, his Radical successors have just begun to realise. Some hints came to him from Condorcet, but most of these daringly novel ideas sprang from Paine's own inventive brain, and all of them are presented by the whilom exciseman, with a wealth of financial detail, as if he were a Chancellor of the Exchequer addressing the first Republican Parliament in the year One of Liberty. He would break up the poor laws, "these instruments of civil torture." He has saved the major part of the cost of defence by a naval alliance with the other Sea Powers, and the abolition of capture at sea. Instead of poor relief he would give a subsidy to the children of the very poor, and pensions to the aged. Four pounds a year for every child under fourteen in every necessitous family will ensure the health and instruction of the next generation. It will cost two millions and a half, but it will banish ignorance. He would pay the costs of compulsory education. Pensions are to be granted not of grace but of right, as an aid to the infirm after fifty years, and a subsidy to the aged after sixty. Maternity benefit is anticipated in a donation of twenty shillings to every poor mother at the birth of a child. Casual labour is to be cared for in some sort of workhouse-factories in London. These reforms are to be financed partly by economies and partly by a graduated income-tax, for which Paine presents an elaborate schedule. When the poor are happy and the jails empty, then at last may a nation boast of its constitution. In this pregnant chapter Paine not only sketched the work of the future ; he exploded his own premises.

The odium that still clings to Paine's theological writings comes mainly from those who have not read them. When Mr. Roosevelt the other day called him " a dirty little Atheist," he exposed nothing but his own ignorance. Paine was a deist, and he wrote *The Age of Reason* on the threshold of a French prison, primarily to counteract the atheism which he thought he saw at work among the Jacobins—an odd diagnosis, for Robespierre was at least as ardent in his deism as Paine himself. He believed in a God, Whose bounty he saw in nature ; he taught the doctrine of conditional immortality, and his quarrel with revealed religion was chiefly that it set up for worship a God of cruelty and injustice. From the stories of the Jewish massacres ordained by divine command, down to the orthodox doctrine of the scheme of redemption, he saw nothing but a history derogatory to the wisdom and goodness of the Almighty. To believe the Old Testament we must unbelieve our faith in the moral justice of God. It might "hurt the stubbornness of a priest" to destroy this fiction, but it would tranquilise the consciences of millions. From this starting-point he proceeds in the later second and third parts to a detailed criticism designed to show that the books of the Bible were not written by their reputed authors, that the miracles are incredible, that the passages claimed as prophecy have been wrested from their contexts, and that many inconsistencies are to be found in the narrative portions of the Gospels.

Acute and fearless though it is, this detailed argument has only an historical interest to-day. When the violence of his persecutors had goaded Paine into anger, he lost all sense of tact in controversy, and lapsed occasionally into harsh vulgarities. But the anger was just, and the zeal for mental honesty has had its reward. Paine had no sense for the mystery and poetry of traditional religion. But what he attacked was not presented to him as poetry. He was assailing a dogmatic orthodoxy which had itself converted poetry into literal fact. As literal fact it was incredible; and Paine, taking it all at the valuation of its own professors, assailed it with a disbelief as prosaic as their belief, but intellectually more honest. His interpretation of the Bible is unscientific, if you will, but it is nearer to the truth of history than the conventional belief of his day. If his polemics seem rough and superfluous to us, it is only because his direct frontal attacks forced on the work of Biblical criticism, and long ago compelled the abandonment of most of the positions which he assailed. In spite of its grave faults of taste and temper and manner, *The Age of Reason* performed an indispensable service to honesty and morals. It was the bravest thing he did, for it threatened his name with an immortality of libel. His place in history is secure at last. The neglected pioneer of one revolution, the honoured victim of another, brave to the point of folly, and as humane as he was brave, no man in his generation preached republican virtue in better English, nor lived it with a finer disregard of self.

CHAPTER III

WILLIAM GODWIN AND THE REVOLUTION

TOM PAINE is still reviled and still admired. The name of Mary Wollstonecraft is honoured by the growing army of free women. Both may be read in cheap editions. William Godwin, a more powerful intellect, and in his day a greater influence than either, is now forgotten, or remembered only because he was the father of Shelley's wife. Yet he blazed in the last decade of the eighteenth century, as Hazlitt has told us, " as a sun in the firmament of reputation." " No one was more talked of, more looked up to, more sought after, and wherever liberty, truth, justice was the theme, his name was not far off. . . . No work in our time gave such a blow to the philosophical mind of the country as the celebrated *Enquiry Concerning Political Justice*. Tom Paine was considered for the time as a Tom Fool to him ; Paley an old woman ; Edmund Burke a flashy sophist."

William Godwin came into the world in

GODWIN AND THE REVOLUTION 79

1756, at Wisbech, in the Fen country, with the moral atmosphere of a dissenting home for inheritance. His father and grandfather were Independent ministers, who taught the metaphysical dissent of the extreme Calvinistic tradition. The quaint ill-spelled letters of his mother reveal a strong character, a meagre education and rigid beliefs. William was unwholesomely precocious as a boy, pious, studious and greedy for distinction and praise. He was brought up on the *Account of the Pious Deaths of Many Godly Children*, and would move his school-fellows to tears by his early sermons on the Last Judgment. At seventeen we find him, destined for the hereditary profession, a student in the Theological College at Hoxton. His mental development was by no means headlong, but he was a laborious reader and an eager disputant, endowed with all the virtues save modesty.

He emerged from College as he had entered it, a Tory in politics and a Sandemanian in religion. The Sandemanians were super-Calvinists, and their tenets may be summarily defined. A Calvinist held that of ten souls nine will be damned. A Sandemanian hoped that of ten Calvinists one may with difficulty be saved. In the Calvinist mould Godwin's mind was formed, and if the doctrine was soon discarded, the habit of thought characteristic of Calvinism remained with him to the end. It is a French and not a British creed, Latin in its systematic completeness, Latin in the logical courage with which it pursues its assumptions to their last conclusion, Latin in its faith in deductive reasoning and its disdain alike of experience and of sentiment. Had Godwin been bred a Methodist or a Churchman, he could not have written *Political Justice*. To him in these early years religion presented itself as a supernatural despotism based on terror and coercion. Its central doctrine was eternal punishment, and when in mature life, Godwin became a free-thinker, his revolt was not so much the readjustment of a speculative thinker who has reconsidered untenable dogmas, as the rebellion of a humane and liberal mind against a system of terrorism. To some agnostics God is an unnecessary hypothesis. To Godwin He was rather a tyrant to be deposed. It was a view which Shelley with less provocation adopted with even greater heat.

Godwin's firm dogmatic creed began to crumble away during his early experiences as a dissenting minister in country towns. He published a forgotten volume of sermons, and his development both in politics and

GODWIN AND THE REVOLUTION

theology was evidently slow. At twenty-seven, as a young pastor at Beaconsfield, we find him a Whig and a Unitarian, who looked up to Dr. Priestley as his master. He had now begun to study the French philosophers, whom Hoxton had doubtless refuted, but did not read. He was not a successful pastor, and it was as much his relative failure in the pulpit as his slowly broadening beliefs which caused him to take to letters for a livelihood. His long literary career begins in 1783 with some years of prentice work in Grub Street. He wrote a successful pamphlet in defence of the Coalition, which brought him to the notice of the Whig chiefs, worked with enthusiasm at a *Life of Chatham* which has the merit of a rather heavy eloquence, contributed for seven years to the *Annual Register* and wrote three novels which evidently enjoyed an ephemeral success. He lived the usual nomadic life of the young man of letters, and differed from most of his kind chiefly by his industry, his abstinence, and his methodical habits of study, which he never relaxed even when he was writing busily for bread.

We find him rising early, and reading some portion of a Greek or Latin classic before breakfast. He acquired by this practice a literary knowledge of the classics and used it in his later essays with an ease and intimacy which many a scholar would envy. He wrote for three or four hours in the morning, composing slowly and frequently recasting his drafts. The afternoon and evening were devoted to eager converse and hot debate with friends, and to the reading of modern books in English, French and Italian, with not infrequent visits to the theatre. A brief diary carefully kept with a system of signs and abbreviations in a queer mixed jargon of English, French and Latin records his anxious use of his time, and shows to the end of his eighty years few wasted days. If industry was his most conspicuous virtue, he gave proof at the outset of his life of an independence rare among poor men who have their career to make. Sheridan, who acted as the literary agent of the Whigs, wished to engage him as a professional pamphleteer and offered him a regular salary. He refused to tie himself to a party, though his views at this time were those of an orthodox and enthusiastic admirer of Fox.

Godwin was to become the apostle of Universal Benevolence. It was a virtue for which in later life he gave many an opportunity to his richer friends, but if he stimulated it in others he never refused to practise it himself.

While he was still a struggling and underpaid journeyman author, wandering from one cheap lodging to another, he burdened himself with the care and maintenance of a distant relative, an orphaned second-cousin, named Thomas Cooper. Cooper came to him at the age of twelve and remained with him till he became an actor at seventeen. Godwin had read Rousseau's *Emile*, not seldom with dissent, and all through his life was deeply interested in the problems of education. They furnished him with the themes of some of the best essays in his *Enquirer* and his *Thoughts on Man*, and young Cooper was evidently the subject on whom he experimented. He was a difficult, proud, high-spirited lad, and the process of tuition was clearly not as smooth as it was conscientious. Godwin's leading thought was that the utmost reverence is due to boys. He cared little how much he imparted of scholastic knowledge. He aimed at arousing the intellectual curiosity of his charge and fostering independence and self-respect. Sincerity and plain-speaking were to govern the relation of tutor and pupil. Corporal punishment was of course a prohibited barbarity, but it must be admitted that in Godwin's case a violent tongue and an impatient temper more than supplied its place. The diary shows how pathetically the tutor exhorted himself to avoid sternness, " which can only embitter the temper," and not to impute dulness, stupidity or intentional error. Some letters show how he failed. Cooper complains that Godwin had called him " a foolish wretch," " a viper " and a " tiger." Godwin replies by complimenting him on his " sensibility," and his " independence," asks for his " confidence " in return, and assures him that he does not expect " gratitude " (a virtue banned in the Godwinian ethics). This essay in education can have been only relatively successful, for Cooper seems to have felt a quite commonplace gratitude to Godwin, and for many a year afterwards sent him vivacious letters, which testify to the real friendship which united them.

Imperious and hot-tempered though he was, Godwin made friends and kept them. Thomas Holcroft came into Godwin's life in 1786. Thanks to Hazlitt's spirited memoir, based as it was on ample autobiographical notes, no personality of this group stands before us so clearly limned, and there is none more attractive. Mrs. Shelley describes him as a " man of stern and irascible character," but he was also lovable and affectionate. There was in his mind and will some powerful

GODWIN AND THE REVOLUTION 85

initial force of resolve and mental independence. He thought for himself, and yet he could assimilate the ideas of other men. He was a reasoner and a doctrinaire; and yet he must have had in himself those untamed volcanic emotions which we associate with the heroes of the romantic novels of the age. He believed in the almost unlimited powers of the human mind, and his own career, which saw his rise from stable-boy and cobbler to dramatist, was itself a monument to the human will. Looking in their mirrors, the progressives of that generation were tempted to think that perfection might have been within their reach had not their youth been stunted by the influence of Calvin and the British Constitution. Rectitude, courage and unflinching truth were Holcroft's ideal. He firmly believed (an idea which lay in germ in Condorcet and was for a time adopted by Godwin) that the will guided by reason might transform not only the human mind but the human body. Like the Christian Scientists of to-day he asserted, as Mrs. Shelley tells us, that " death and disease existed only through the feebleness of man's mind, that pain also had no reality."

He was a man of fifty when he met Godwin at thirty, and he had packed into his half century a more various experience of men and things than the studious and sedentary Godwin could have acquired if he had lived the life of the Wandering Jew. Theirs was a friendship of mutual stimulation and intimate exchange which is commoner between a man and a woman than between two men. They met almost daily, and in spite of some violent lovers' quarrels, their affection lasted till Holcroft's death in 1809. It is not hard to understand their quarrels. Neither of them had natural tact, and Godwin's sensibility was morbid. Unflinching truthfulness, even in literary criticism, must have tried their tempers, and the single word " démêlé," best translated " row," occurs often in Godwin's diary as his note on one of their meetings. It is not easy to decide which influenced the other more. Godwin's was the trained, systematic, academical mind, but Holcroft added to a rich and curious experience of life and a vein of native originality, wide reading and something more than a mere amateur's taste for music and art. It was Holcroft who drove Godwin out of his compromising Unitarianism into a view which for some years he boldly described as Atheism. His religious opinions were afterwards modified (or so he supposed) by S. T. Coleridge; but that

GODWIN AND THE REVOLUTION 87

influence is not conspicuous in his posthumous essay on religion, and the best label for his attitude is perhaps Huxley's word, " Agnostic."

As the French Revolution approached, the two friends fell under the prevailing excitement. Godwin attended the Revolution Society's dinners, and Holcroft was, as we have seen, a leading member of the Corresponding Society. There is no difficulty in accounting for most of the opinions which the two friends held in common, and which Godwin was soon to embody in *Political Justice*. Some were common to all the group; others lie in germ at least in the writings of the Encyclopædists. Even communism was anticipated by Mably, and was held in some tentative form by many of the leading men of the Revolution. (See Kropotkin: *The Great French Revolution*.) The puzzle is rather to account for the anarchist tendency which seems to be wholly original in Godwin. It was a revolt not merely against all coercive action by the State, but also against collective action by the citizens. The root of it was probably the extreme individualism which felt that a man surrendered too much of himself, too much of truth and manhood in any political association. The beginnings of this line of thought may be detected in a vivid contemptuous account of the riotous Westminster election of 1788, in which Holcroft had worked with the Foxites : " Scandal, pitiful, mean, mutual scandal, never was more plentifully dispersed. Electioneering is a trade so despicably degrading, so eternally incompatible with moral and mental dignity that I can scarcely believe a truly great mind capable of the dirty drudgery of such vice. I am at least certain no mind is great while thus employed. It is the periodical reign of the evil nature or demon."

This, to be sure, is no more than a hint of a tendency, but it shows that experience was already fermenting in the brain of one member at least of the pair, and it took these alchemists no great while to distil from it their theoretic spirit. The doings of the Corresponding Society were destined to enlarge and confirm this experience. In the hopes, the indignations, and the perils of the years of revolutionary excitement Godwin had his intimate share. He was one of a small committee which undertook the publication of Paine's *Rights of Man*, and when the repression began, those who were struck down were his associates and in some cases his intimates. Holcroft, as we have seen, was tried for high treason, and Joseph Gerrald, who was sent to

Botany Bay, was a friend for whom he felt both admiration and affection. If the fate of these men was a haunting pain to their friends, their high courage and idealistic faith was a noble stimulus. " Human Perfectibility " had its martyrs, and the words of Gerrald as he stood in the dock awaiting the sentence that was to send him to his death among thieves and forgers, deserve a respectful record : " Moral light is as irresistible by the mind as physical by the eye. All attempts to impede its progress are vain. It will roll rapidly along, and as well may tyrants imagine that by placing their feet upon the earth they can stop its diurnal motion, as that they shall be able by efforts the most virulent and pertinacious to extinguish the light of reason and philosophy, which happily for mankind is everywhere spreading around us." It was in this atmosphere of enthusiasm and devotion that *Political Justice* was written.

The main work of Godwin's life was begun in July, 1791. He was fortunate in securing a contract from the publisher Robinson, on generous terms which ultimately brought him in one thousand guineas. *Political Justice* has been generally classed among the answers to Burke, but Godwin's aim was in fact something more ambitious. A note in his diary deserves to be quoted: " My original conception proceeded on a feeling of the imperfections and errors of Montesquieu, and a desire of supplying a less faulty work. In the just fervour of my enthusiasm I entertained the vain imagination of " hewing a stone from the rock," which by its inherent energy and weight, should overbear and annihilate all opposition and place the principles of politics on an immoveable basis."

When he came to answer his critics, he apologised for extravagances on the plea of haste and excitement; but in fact the work was slowly and deliberately written, and was not completed until January, 1793. Its doctrines, since the book is not now readily accessible, will be summarised fully and in Godwin's own phraseology in the next chapter, but it seems proper to draw attention here to the cool yet unprovocative courage of its writer. It is filled with " hanging matters." Pitt was, perhaps, no more disposed to punish a man for expounding the fundamental principles of philosophic anarchism than was the Russian autocracy in our own day when it tolerated Tolstoy. It was not for writing *Utopia* that Sir Thomas More lost his head. But the book is quite unflinching in its application of principle, and its attacks on monarchy are as uncompromising as those for which Paine was outlawed. The preface calmly discusses the possibility of prosecution, issues what is in effect a quiet challenge, and concludes with the consolation that " it is the property of truth to be fearless and to prove victorious over every adversary." The fact was that Godwin watched the dangers of his friends " almost with envy " (letter to Gerrald). But he held that a man who deliberately provokes martyrdom acts immorally, since he confuses the progress of reason by exciting destructive passions, and drives his adversaries into evil courses.

" For myself," he wrote, " I will never adopt any conduct for the express purpose of being put upon my trial, but if I be ever so put, I will consider that day as a day of triumph." Godwin escaped punishment for his activity on behalf of Holcroft and the twelve reformers, because his activity was successful. He escaped prosecution for *Political Justice* because it was a learned book, addressed to educated readers, and issued at the astonishing price of three guineas. The propriety of prosecuting him was considered by the Privy Council; and Pitt is said to have dismissed the suggestion with the remark that " a three guinea book could never do much harm among those who had not three shillings to spare." That this three-guinea book was bought and read to the extent of no less than four thousand copies is a tribute not merely to its vitality, but to the eagerness of the middle-classes during the revolutionary ferment to drink in the last words of the new philosophy.

A new edition was soon called for, and was issued early in 1796. Much of the book was recast and many chapters entirely rewritten, as the consequence not so much of any material change in Godwin's views, as of the profit he had derived from private controversies. Condorcet (though he is never mentioned) is, if one may make a guess, the chief of the new influences apparent in the second edition. It is more cautious, more visibly the product of a varied experience than the first draft, but it abandons none of his leading ideas. A third edition appeared in 1799, toned down still further by a growing caution. These revisions undoubtedly made the book less interesting, less vivid, less readable. No modern edition has ever appeared, and its direct influence had become negligible even before Godwin's death. It is harder to account for the oblivion into which the book has fallen, than to explain its early popularity. It is not a difficult book to read. " The young and

GODWIN AND THE REVOLUTION

the fair," Godwin tells us, " did not feel deterred from consulting my pages." His style is always clear and often eloquent. His vocabulary seems to a modern taste overloaded with Latin words, but the architecture of his sentences is skilful in the classical manner. He can vary his elaborate periods with a terse, strong statement which comes with the force of an unexpected blow. He has a knack of happy illustration, and a way of enforcing his points by putting problems in casuistry which have an alluring human interest. The book moved his own generation profoundly, and even to-day his more enthusiastic passages convey an irresistible impression of sincerity and conviction.

CHAPTER IV

"POLITICAL JUSTICE"

THE controversy which produced *Political Justice* was a dialogue between the future and the past. The task of speculation in England had been, through a stagnant century, to define the conditions of political stability, and to admire the elaborate checks and balances of the British Constitution as though change were the only evil that threatened mankind. For Burke, change itself was but an incident in the triumph of continuity and conservation. For Godwin the whole life of mankind is a race through innovation to perfection, and his main concern is to exhort the athlete to fling aside the garments of prejudice, tradition, and constraint, until one asks at the end how much of flesh and blood has been torn away with the garments. If one were to attempt in a phrase to sum up his work, the best title which one could invent for it would be Prolegomena to all Future Progress. What in a word are the conditions of progress?

"POLITICAL JUSTICE" 95

His attitude to mankind is by turns a pedagogue's disapprobation and a patron's encouragement. The worst enemy of progress was the systematic optimism of Leibnitz and Pope, which Voltaire had overthrown. There is indeed enough of progress in the past to fire our courage and our hopes. In moments of depression, he would admire the beautiful invention of writing and the power of mind displayed in human speech. But the general panorama of history exhorts us to fundamental change. In bold sweeping rhetoric he assures us that history is little else than the record of crime. War has diminished neither its horror nor its frequency, and man is still the most formidable enemy to man. Despotism is still the fate of the greatest part of mankind. Penal laws by the terror of punishment hold a numerous class in abject penury. Robbery and fraud are none the less continual, and the poor are tempted for ever to violence against the more fortunate. One person in seven comes in England on the poor rates. Can the poor conceive of society as a combination to protect every man in his rights and secure him the means of existence ? Is it not rather for them a conspiracy to engross its advantages for the favoured few ? Luxury insults them ; admiration is the exclusive property of the rich, and contempt the constant lacquey of poverty. Nowhere is a man valued for what he is. Legislation aggravates the natural inequality of man. A house of landlords sets to work to deprive the poor of the little commonage of nature which remained to them, and its bias stands revealed when we recollect that in England (as Paine had pointed out) while taxes on land produce half a million less than they did a century ago, taxes on articles of general consumption produce thirteen millions more. Robbery is a capital offence because the poor alone are tempted to it. Among the poor alone is all combination forbidden. Godwin was often an incautious rhetorician. He painted the present in colours of such unrelieved gloom, that it is hard to see in it the possibility of a brighter future. Mankind seems hopeless, and he has to prove it perfectible.

Are these evils then the necessary condition of society ? Godwin answers that question as the French school, and in particular Helvétius, had done, by a preliminary assault on the assumptions of a reactionary philosophy. He proposes to exhort the human will to embark with a conscious and social resolve on the adventure of perfection. He must first demonstrate that the will is sovereign. Man is the creature of necessity, and the nexus of cause and effect governs the moral world like the physical. We are the product of our conditions. But among conditions some are within the power of the will to change and others are not. Montesquieu had insisted that it is climate which ultimately differentiates the races of mankind. Climate is clearly a despotism which we can never hope to reform away. Another school has taught that men come into the world with innate ideas and a predetermined character. Others again would dispute that man is in his actions a reasonable being, and would represent him as the toy of passion, a creature to whom it is useless to present an argument drawn from his own advantage. The first task of the progressive philosopher is to clear away these preliminary obstacles. Man is the creature of conditions, but primarily of those conditions which he may hope to modify— education, religion, social prejudice and above all government. He is also in the last resort a being whose conduct is governed by his opinions. Admit these premises and the way is clear towards perfection. It is a problem which in some form and in some dialect confronts every generation of reformers. We are the creatures of our own environment, but in some degree we are ourselves a force which can modify that environment. We inherit a past which weighs upon us and obsesses us, but in some degree each generation is born anew. Godwin used the new psychology against the old superstition of innate ideas. A modern thinker in his place would advance Weissmann's biological theory that the acquired modifications of an organism are not inherited, as an answer to the pessimism which bases itself upon heredity.

Godwin starts boldly with the thesis that " the characters of men originate in their external circumstances." He brushes aside innate ideas or instincts or even ante-natal impressions. Accidents in the womb may have a certain effect, and every man has a certain disposition at birth. But the multiplicity of later experiences wears out these early impressions. Godwin, in all this, reproduces the current fallacy of his generation. Impressions and experiences were for them something external, flung upon the surface of the mind. They were just beginning to realise that the mind works when it perceives. Change a nobleman's child at birth with a ploughman's, and each will grow up quite naturally in his new circumstances. Exercise makes the muscles ; education, argument, and the exchange of opinion the mind. " It is impression that makes the man, and compared with the empire of impression, the mere differences of animal structure are inexpressibly unimportant and powerless." Change continues through life ; everything mental and physical is in flux ; why suppose that only in the propensities of the new-born infant is there something permanent and inflexible ? Helvétius had been Godwin's chief precursor in this opinion. He had gone so far as to declare that men are at birth equal, some raw human stuff which " education," in the broad sense of the word, proceeds to modify in the long schooling from the cradle to the grave. Men differ in genius, he would assert, by education and experience, not by natural organisation. The original acuteness of the senses has little to do with the development of talent. The new psychology had swept " faculties " away. Interest is the main factor in the development of perception and attention. The scarcity of attention is the true cause of the scarcity of genius, and the chief means of promoting it are emulation and the love of glory.

Godwin is too cautious to accept this ultra-revolutionary statement of the potential equality of men without some reserves. But the idea inspires him as it inspired all the vital thought of his day. It set humane physicians at the height of the Terror to work on discovering a method by which even defective and idiot children might be raised by "education" to the normal stature of the human mind. It fired Godwin himself with a zeal for education. "Folly," said Helvétius, "is factitious." "Nature," said Godwin, "never made a dunce." The failures of education are due primarily to the teacher's error in substituting compulsion for persuasion and despotism for encouragement. The excellences and defects of the human character are not due to occult causes beyond the reach of ingenuity to modify or correct, nor are false views the offspring of an irresistible destiny. Our conventional schools are the slaughter-houses of mind; but of all the external influences which build up character and opinion, the chief are political. It is Godwin's favourite theme, and he carries it even further than Holbach and Helvétius had done. From this influence there is no escape, for it infects the teacher no less than the taught. Equality will make men frank, ingenuous and intrepid, but a great disparity of ranks renders men cold, irresolute, timid and cautious. However lofty the morality of the teacher, the mind of the child is continually corrupted by seeing, in the society around him, wealth honoured, poverty contemned, intrepid virtue proscribed and servility encouraged. From the influence of social and political institutions there is no escape: "They poison our minds before we can resist or so much as suspect their malignity. Like the barbarous directors of Eastern seraglios they deprive us of our virility, and fit us for their despicable employment from the cradle. So false is the opinion that has too generally prevailed that politics is an affair with which ordinary men have little concern."

Here Godwin is introducing into English thinking an idea originally French. English writers from Locke to Paine had spoken of government as something purely negative, so little important that only when a man saw his property threatened or his shores invaded, was he forced to recollect that he had a country. Godwin saw its influence everywhere, insinuating itself into our personal dispositions and insensibly communicating its spirit to our private transactions. The idea in his hands made for hope. Reform, or better still, abolish governments, and to what heights of virtue might not men aspire? We need not say with Rousseau that men are naturally virtuous. The child, as Helvétius delighted to point out, will do that for a coral or a doll which he will do at a mature age for a title or a sceptre. Men are rather the infinitely malleable, variable stuff on which education and persuasion can play.

The first essential dogma of perfectibility, the first presupposition of progress is, then, that men's characters depend on external circumstances. The second dogma, the second condition of hope is that the voluntary actions of men originate in their opinions. It is an orthodox Socratic position, but Godwin was not a student of Plato. He laid down this dogma as the necessary basis of any reform by persuasion. There is much virtue in the word "voluntary." In so far as actions are voluntary, the doctrine is self-evident. A voluntary action is accompanied by foresight, and the idea of certain consequences is its motive. A judgment "this is good" or "this is desirable," has preceded the action, and it originates therefore in an opinion however fugitive. In moments of passion my attention is so engrossed by a particular view of the subject that I forget considerations by which I am commonly guided. Even in battles between reason and sense, he holds, the contending forces assume

"POLITICAL JUSTICE" 103

a rational form. It is opinion contending with opinion and judgment with judgment. At this point the modern reader will become sceptical. These internal struggles assume a rational form only when self-consciousness reviews them—that is to say when they are over. In point of fact, Godwin argues, sheer sensuality has a smaller empire over us than we commonly suppose. Strip the feast of its social pleasures, and the commerce of the sexes of all its intellectual and emotional allurements, and who would be overcome?

One need not follow Godwin minutely in his handling of what is after all a commonplace of academic philosophy. He was concerned to insist that men's voluntary actions originate in opinion, that he might secure a fulcrum for the leverage of argument and persuasion. Vice is error, and error can always be corrected " Show me in the clearest and most unambiguous manner that a certain mode of proceeding is most reasonable in itself, or most conducive to my interest, and I shall infallibly pursue that mode, so long as the views you suggested to me continue present to my mind." The practical problem is therefore to make ourselves and our fellows perfectly conscious of our motives, and always prepared to render a reason for our actions. The perfection of human character is to approach as nearly as possible to the absolutely voluntary state, to act always, in other words, from a clear and comprehensive survey of the consequences which we desire to produce.

The incautious reader may be invited to pause at this point, for in this premise lies already the whole of philosophic anarchism. You have admitted that voluntary action is rational. You have conceded that all action *ought* to be voluntary. The silent assumption is that by education and effort it *can* be made so. One may doubt whether in the sense required by Godwin's argument any human action ever is or can be absolutely "voluntary," rational or self-conscious. To attain it, we should have to reason naked in a desert with algebraic symbols. To use words is to think in step, and to beg our question. But Godwin is well aware that most men rarely reason. He is here framing an ideal, without realising its remoteness. The mischief of his faith in logic as a force, was that it led him to ignore the æsthetic and emotional influences, by which the mass of men can best be led to a virtuous ideal. Shelley, who was a thorough Platonist, supplements, as we shall see (p. 234), this characteristic defect in his master's teach-

"POLITICAL JUSTICE" 105

ing. The main conclusions follow rapidly. Sound reasoning and truth when adequately communicated must always be victorious over error. Truth, then, is omnipotent, and the vices and moral weaknesses of man are not invincible. Man, in short, is perfectible, or in other words, susceptible of perpetual improvement. These sentiments have to the modern ear a platitudinous ring. So far from being platitudes, they are explosives capable of destroying the whole fabric of government. For if truth is omnipotent, why trust to laws ? If men will obey argument, why use constraint ?

But let us move slowly towards this extreme conclusion. If reason appears to-day to play but a feeble part in society, and exerts only a limited empire over the actions of men, it is because unlettered ignorance, social habits and the positive institutions of government stand in the way. Where the masses of mankind are sunk in brutal ignorance, one need not wonder that argument and persuasion have but a small influence with them. Truth indeed is rarely recondite or difficult to communicate. Godwin might have quoted Helvétius : " It is with genius as with an astronomer ; he sees a new star and forthwith all can see it." Nor need we fear the objection that by introducing an intellectual element into virtue, we have removed it beyond the reach of simple men. A virtuous action, indeed, must be good both in intention and in tendency. Godwin was like Helvétius and Priestley, a Utilitarian in ethics, and defined duty as that mode of action on the part of the individual which constitutes the best possible application of his capacity to the general benefit, in every situation that presents itself. One may be mistaken as to what will contribute to the general benefit, as Sir Everard Digby was, for example, when he thought it his duty to blow up King James and the Parliament. But the simple man need be at no loss. An earnest desire will in some degree generate capacity. There Godwin opened a profoundly interesting and stimulating line of thought. The mind is formed not by its innate powers, but by its governing desires. As love brings eloquence to the suitor, so if I do but ardently desire to serve my kind, I shall find out a way, and while I study a plan shall find that my faculties have been exercised and increased. Moreover, in the struggle after virtue I am not alone.

Burke made the first of the virtues prudence. Godwin would have given sincerity that place.

"POLITICAL JUSTICE"

To him and his circle the chief business of social converse was by argument and exhortation to strengthen the habit of virtue. There was something to be said for the practice of auricular confession; but how much better would it be if every man were to make the world his confessional and the human species the keeper of his conscience. The practice of sincerity would give to our conversation a Roman boldness and fervour. The frank distribution of praise and blame is the most potent incentive to virtue. Were we but bold and impartial in our judgments, vice would be universally deserted and virtue everywhere practised. Our cowardice in censure and correction is the chief reason of the perpetuation of abuses. If every man would tell all the truth he knew, it is impossible to predict how short would be the reign of usurpation and folly. Let our motive be philanthropy, and we need not fear ruggedness or brutality, disdain or superiority, since we aim at the interest of him we correct, and not at the triumph of the corrector. In an aside Godwin demands the abolition of social conventions which offend sincerity. If I must deny myself to a visitor, I should scorn the polite lie that I am "not at home."

It is a consequence also of this doctrine,

that there should be no prosecutions for libel, even in private matters. Truth depends on the free shock of opinions, and the unrestrained discussion of private character is almost as important as freedom in speculative enquiry. "If the truth were universally told of men's dispositions and actions, gibbets and wheels might be dismissed from the face of the earth. The knave unmasked would be obliged to turn honest in his own defence. Nay, no man would have time to turn a knave. Truth would follow him in his first irresolute essays, and public disapprobation arrest him in the commencement of his career." It is shameful for a good man to retort on a slander, "I will have recourse to the only means that are congenial to guilt: I will compel you to be silent." Freedom in this matter, as in all others, will engender activity and fortitude; positive institution (Godwin's term for law and constraint) makes the mind torpid and lethargic. It is hardly necessary to reproduce Godwin's vigorous arguments for unfettered freedom in political and speculative discussion, against censorships and prosecutions for religious and political opinions. Even were we secure from the possibility of mistake, mischief and not good would accrue from the attempt to impose our

"POLITICAL JUSTICE" 109

infallible opinions upon our neighbours. Men deserve approbation only in so far as they are independent in their opinions and free in their actions.

Equally clear is it that the establishment of religion and all systems of tests must be abolished. They make for hypocrisy, check advance in speculation, and teach us to estimate a disinterested sincerity at a cheap rate. We need not fear disorder as a consequence of complete liberty of speech. "Arguments alone will not have the power, unassisted by the sense or the recollection of oppression or treachery to hurry the people into excesses. Excesses are never the offspring of speculative reason, are never the offspring of misrepresentation only, but of power endeavouring to stifle reason, and to traverse the commonsense of mankind."

A more original deduction from Godwin's demand for the unlimited freedom of opinion, was that he objected vehemently to any system of national education. Condorcet had drawn up a marvellously complete project for universal compulsory education, with full liberty indeed for the teachers, whose technical competence alone the State would guarantee, and with a scheme of free scholarships, an educational "ladder" more generous than anything which has yet been realised in fact. Godwin objects that State-regulated institutions will stereotype knowledge and make for an undesirable permanence and uniformity in opinion. They diffuse what is known and forget what remains to be known. They erect a system of authority and separate a tenet from the evidence on which it rests, so that beliefs cease to be perceptions and become prejudices. No Government is to be trusted with the dangerous power to create and regulate opinions through its schools. Such a power is, indeed, more dangerous than that of an Established Church, and would be used to strengthen tyranny and perpetuate faulty institutions.

Godwin, needless to say, takes, as did Condorcet, the side of frankness in the controversy which was a test of democratic faith in this generation—whether " political imposture " is allowable, and whether a statesman should encourage the diffusion of " salutary prejudices " among the unlearned, the poor and women. This was indeed the main eighteenth century defence for monarchy and aristocracy. Kings and governors are not wiser than other men, but it is useful that they should be thought so. Such imposture, Godwin argued, is as futile as the parallel use by religion of the pains and penalties of the afterworld. It is the sober who are demoralised by it, and not the lawless who are deterred. To terrify men is a strange way of rendering them judicious, fearless and happy. It is to leave men indolent and unbraced by truth. He objects even to the trappings and ceremonies which are used to render magistrates outwardly venerable and awe-inspiring, so that they may impress the irrational imagination. These means may be used as easily to support injustice as to render justice acceptable. They divide men into two classes; those who may reason, and those who must take everything on trust. This is to degrade them both. The masses are kept in perpetual vibration between rebellious discontent and infatuated credulity. And can we suppose that the practice of concealment and hypocrisy will make no breaches in the character of the governing class?

The general effect of any meddling of authority with opinion is that the mind is robbed of its genuine employment. Such a system produces beings wanting in independence, and in that intrepid perseverance and calm self-approbation which grow from independence. Such beings are the mere dwarfs and mockeries of men.

Godwin was at issue here as much with Rousseau as with Burke, but his trust in the people, it should be explained, was based rather on faith in what they might become, than on admiration for what they were.

That all government is an evil, though doubtless a necessary evil, was the typical opinion of the individualistic eighteenth century. It would not long have survived such proposals as Paine's scheme of old age pensions and Condorcet's project of national education. When men have perceived that an evil can be turned to good account, they are already on the road which will lead them to discard their premises. But Godwin was quite unaffected by this new Liberalism. No positive good was to be hoped from government, and much positive evil would flow from it at the best. In his absolute individualism he went further. The whole idea of government was radically wrong. For him the individual was tightly enclosed in his own skin, and any constraint was an infringement of his personality. He would have poured scorn on the half-mystical conception of a social organism. Nor did it occur to him that a man might voluntarily subject himself to government, losing none of his own autonomy in the act, from a persuasion that government

"POLITICAL JUSTICE" 113

is on the whole a benefit, and that submission, even when his own views are thwarted, is a free man's duty within certain limits, accepted gladly for the sake of preserving an institution which commonly works well. He did not see the institution working well; he did not believe in the benefits; he was convinced that more than all the advantages of the best of governments could be obtained from the free operation of opinion in an unorganised community.

His main point is lucidly simple. It was an application of the Whig and Protestant doctrine of the right of private judgment. "If in any instance I am made the mechanical instrument of absolute violence, in that instance I fall under a pure state of external slavery." Nor is the case much better, if instead of waiting for the actual application of coercion, I act in obedience to authority from the hope and fear of the State's rewards and punishments. For virtue has ceased, and I am acting from self-interest. It is a triviality to distinguish, as Whig thinkers do, between matters of conscience (in which the State should not meddle) and my conduct in the civil concerns of daily life (which the State should regulate). What sort of moralist can he be, who makes no conscience of what he does in his daily intercourse with other men? " I have deeply reflected upon the nature of virtue, and am convinced that a certain proceeding is incumbent on me. But the hangman supported by an Act of Parliament assures me that I am mistaken. If I yield my opinion to his dictum, my action becomes modified, and my character also. . . . Countries exposed to the perpetual interference of decrees instead of arguments, exhibit within their boundaries the mere phantoms of men."

The root of the whole matter is that brute force is an offence against reason, and an unnecessary offence, if in fact men are guided by opinion and will yield to argument. " The case of punishment is the case of you and me differing in opinion, and your telling me that you must be right since you have a more brawny arm."

If I must obey, it is better and less demoralising to yield an external submission so as to escape penalty or constraint, than to yield to authority from a general confidence which enslaves the mind. Comply but criticise. Obey but beware of reverence. If I surrender my conscience to another man's keeping, I annihilate my individuality as a man, and become the ready tool of him among my

"POLITICAL JUSTICE" 115

neighbours who shall excel in imposture and artifice. I put an end moreover to the happy collision of understandings upon which the hopes of human improvement depend. Governments depend upon the unlimited confidence of their subjects, and confidence rests upon ignorance.

Government (has not Burke said so ?) is the perpetual enemy of change, and prompts us to seek the public welfare not in alteration and improvement, but in a timid reverence for the decisions of our ancestors, as if it were the nature of the human mind always to degenerate and never to advance. Godwin thought with John Bright, " We stand on the shoulders of our forefathers—and see further."

In proportion as weakness and ignorance shall diminish, the basis of government will also decay. That will be its true euthanasia.

There is indeed nothing to be said for government save that for a time, and within jealously drawn limits, it may be a fatal and indispensable necessity. A just government cannot be founded on force: for force has no affinity with justice. It cannot be based upon the will of God ; we have no revelation that recommends one form of government rather than another. As little can it be based upon contract. Who were the parties to the

116   SHELLEY AND GODWIN

pretended social contract ? For whom did they consent, for themselves or for their descendants, and to how great a variety of propositions ? Have I assented or my ancestors for me, to the laws of England in fifty volumes folio, and to all that shall hereafter be added to them ? In a few contemptuous pages Godwin buries the social contract. Men when they digest the articles of a contract are not empowered to create rights, but only to declare what was previously right. But the doctrine of the natural rights of man fares no better at his hands. There is no such thing as a positive right to do as we list. One way of acting in every emergency is reasonable, and the other is not. One way will benefit mankind, and the other will not. It is a pestilent doctrine and a denial of all virtue, to say that we have a right to do what we will with our own. Everything we possess has a destination prescribed to it by the immutable voice of reason and justice.

Duties and rights are correlative. As it cannot be the duty of men or societies to do anything to the detriment of human happiness, so it appears with equal evidence that they cannot have the right to do so. There cannot be a more absurd proposition than that which affirms the right of doing wrong. The voice of the people is not the voice of God, nor does universal consent or a majority vote convert wrong into right. It is absurd to say that any set of people has a right to set up any form of government it chooses, or any sect to establish any superstition however detestable. All this would have delighted Burke, but Godwin stands firmly in his path by asserting what he calls the one negative right of man. It is in a word, the right to exercise virtue, the right to a region of choice, a sphere of discretion, which his neighbours must not infringe save by censure and remonstrance. When I am constrained, I cease to be a person, and become a thing. " I ought to exercise my talents for the benefit of others, but the exercise must be the fruit of my own conviction ; no man must attempt to press me into the service."

Government is an evil, and the business of human advancement is to dispense with it as rapidly as may be. In the period of transition Godwin had but a secondary interest, and his sketch of it is slight. He dismisses in turn despotism, aristocracy, the "mixed monarchy" of the Whigs, and the president with kingly powers of some American thinkers. His pages on these subjects are vigorous, well-reasoned, and pointed in their satire. It required much courage to write them, but they do not contain his original contribution to political theory. What is most characteristic in his line of argument is his insistence on the moral corruption that monarchy and aristocracy involve. The whole standard of moral values is subverted. To achieve ostentation becomes the first object of desire. Disinterested virtue is first suspected and then viewed with incredulity. Luxury meanwhile distorts our whole attitude to our fellows, and in every effort to excel and shine we wrong the labouring millions. Aristocracy involves general degradation, and can survive only amid general ignorance. " To make men serfs and villeins it is indispensably necessary to make them brutes. . . . A servant who has been taught to write and read, ceases to be any longer a passive machine."

From the abolition of monarchy and aristocracy Godwin, and indeed the whole revolutionary school, expected the cessation of war. War and conquest elevate the few at the expense of the rest, and cannot benefit the whole community. Democracies have no business with war save to repel an invasion of their territory. He thought of patriotism and love of country much as did Dr. Price.

"POLITICAL JUSTICE" 119

They are (as Hervé has argued in our own day) specious illusions invented to render the multitude the blind instruments of crooked designs. We must not be lured into pursuing the general wealth, prosperity or glory of the society to which we belong. Society is an abstraction, an "ideal existence," and is not on its own account entitled to the smallest regard. Let us not be led away into rendering services to society for which no individual man is the better. Godwin is scornful of wars to maintain the balance of power, or to protect our fellow-countrymen abroad. Some proportion must be observed between the evil of which we complain and the evil which the proposed remedy inevitably includes. War may be defensible in support of the liberty of an oppressed people, but let us wait (here he is clearly censuring the practice of the French Republic) until the oppressed people rises. Do not interfere to force it to be free, and do not forget the resources of pacific persuasion. As to foreign possessions there is little to be said. Do without them. Let colonies attend to their own defence ; no State would wish to have colonies if free trade were universal. Liberty is equally good for every race of men, and democracy, since it is founded on reason, a universal form of government. There follow some naïve prescriptions for conducting democratic wars. Sincerity forbids ambuscades and secresy. Never invade, nor assume the offensive. A citizen militia must replace standing armies. Training and discipline are of little value; the ardour of a free people will supply their place.

Godwin's leading idea when he comes to sketch a shadowy constitution is an extreme dislike of overgrown national States. Political speculation in his day idealised the city republic of antiquity. Helvétius, hoping to get rid as far as possible of government, had advocated a system of federated commonwealths, each so small that public opinion and the fear of shame would act powerfully within it. He would have divided France into thirty republics, each returning four deputies to a federal council. The Girondins cherished the same idea, and lost their heads for it. Tolstoy, going back to the village community as the only possible scene of a natural and virtuous life, exhibits the same tendency.

For Godwin the true unit of society is the parish. Neighbours best understand each others' concerns, and in a limited area there is no room for ambition to unfold itself. Great talents will have their sphere outside this little circle in the work of moulding

"POLITICAL JUSTICE"

opinion. Within the parish public opinion is supreme, and acts through juries, which may at first be obliged to exert some degree of violence in dealing with offenders :—" But this necessity does not arise out of the nature of man, but out of the institutions by which he has already been corrupted. Man is not originally vicious. He would not . . . refuse to be convinced by the expostulations that are addressed to him, had he not been accustomed to regard them as hypocritical, and to conceive that while his neighbour, his parent and his political governor pretended to be actuated by a pure regard to his interest or pleasure, they were in reality, at the expense of his, promoting their own. . . . Render the plain dictates of justice level to every capacity . . . and the whole species will become reasonable and virtuous. It will then be sufficient for juries to recommend a certain mode of adjusting controversies, without assuming the prerogative of dictating that adjustment. It will then be sufficient for them to invite offenders to forsake their errors. . . . Where the empire of reason was so universally acknowledged, the offender would either readily yield to the expostulations of authority, or if he resisted, though suffering no personal molestation, he would feel so weary under the unequivocal disapprobation and the observant eye of public judgment as willingly to remove to a society more congenial to his errors." The picture is not so Utopian as it sounds. It is a very fair sketch of the social structure of a Macedonian village community under Turkish rule, with the massacres left out.

For the rest Godwin was reluctantly prepared to admit the wisdom of instituting a single chamber National Assembly, to manage the common affairs of the parishes, to arrange their disputes and to provide for national defence. But it should suffice for it to meet for one day annually or thereabouts. Like the juries it would at first issue commands, but would in time find it sufficient to publish invitations backed by arguments. Godwin, who is quite prepared to idealise his district juries, pours forth an unstinted contempt upon Parliaments and their procedure. They make a show of unanimity where none exists. The prospect of a vote destroys the intellectual value of debate ; the will of one man really dominates, and the existence of party frustrates persuasion. The whole is based upon " that intolerable insult upon all reason and justice, the deciding upon truth by the casting up of numbers." He omits to tell us whether

"POLITICAL JUSTICE" 123

he would allow his juries to vote. Fortunately legislation is unnecessary: "The inhabitants of a small parish living with some degree of that simplicity which best corresponds with the real nature and wants of a human being, would soon be led to suspect that general laws were unnecessary and would adjudge the causes that came before them not according to certain axioms previously written, but according to the circumstances and demand of each particular cause."

Godwin had a clear mental picture of the gradual decay of authority towards the close of the period of transition; his vision of the earlier stages is less definite. He set his faith on the rapid working of enquiry and persuasion, but he does not explain in detail how, for example, we are to rid ourselves of kings. He once met the Prince Regent, but it is not recorded that he talked to him of virtue and equality, as the early Quakers talked to the man Charles Stuart. He is chiefly concerned to warn his revolutionary friends against abrupt changes. There must be a general desire for change, a conviction of the understanding among the masses, before any change is wise. When a whole nation, or even an unquestionable majority of a nation, is resolved on change, no government, even with a standing army behind it, can stand against it. Every reformer imagines that the country is with him. What folly! Even when the majority seems resolved, what is the quality of their resolution? They do, perhaps, sincerely dislike some specific tax. But do they dislike the vice and meanness that grow out of tyranny, and pant for the liberal and ingenuous virtue that would be fostered in their own minds by better conditions? It is a disaster when the unillumined masses are instigated to violent revolution. Revolutions are always crude, bloody, uncertain and inimical to tolerance, independence, and intellectual inquiry. They are a detestable persecution when a minority promotes them. If they must occur, at least postpone them as long as possible. External freedom is worthless without the magnaminity, firmness and energy that should attend it. But if a man have these things, there is little left for him to desire. He cannot be degraded, nor become useless and unhappy. Let us not be in haste to overthrow the usurped powers of the world. Make men wise, and by that very operation you make them free. It is unfortunate that men are so eager to strike and have so little constancy to reason. We should desire neither violent change nor the stagnation that inflames and produces revolutions. Our prayer to governments should be, "Do not give us too soon; do not give us too much; but act under the incessant influence of a disposition to give us something."

These are the reflections of a man who wrote amid the Terror. He had seen the Corresponding Society at work, and the experience made him more than sceptical of any form of association in politics, and led him into a curiously biassed argument, rhetorical in form, forensic in substance. Temporary combinations may be necessary in a time of turmoil, or to secure some single limited end, such as the redress of a wrong done to an individual. Where their scope is general and their duration long continued, they foster declamation, cabal, party spirit and tumult. They are frequented by the artful, the intemperate, the acrimonious, and avoided by the sober, the sceptical, the contemplative citizen. They foster a fallacious uniformity of opinion and render the mind quiescent and stationary. Truth disclaims the alliance of marshalled numbers. The conditions most favourable to reasoned enquiry and calm persuasion are to be found in small and friendly circles. The moral beauty of the spectacle offered by these groups of friends united to pursue truth and foster virtue, will render it contagious. So the craggy steep of science will be levelled and knowledge rendered accessible to all.

The conception of the State which Godwin sought to supplant was itself limited and negative. Government was little else in his day than a means for internal defence against criminals and for external defence against aggression. For the rest, it helped landlords to enclose commons, kept down wages by poor relief and in a muddle-headed way interfered with the freedom of trade. But its central activity was the repression of crime, and for Godwin's system the test question was his handling of the problem of crime and punishment. He was no Platonist, but not for the first time we discover him in a familiar Socratic position. " Do you punish a man," asked Socrates, " to make him better or to make him worse ? " Godwin starts by rejecting the traditional conception of punishment. The word means the infliction of evil upon a vicious being, not merely because the public advantage demands it, but because there is a certain fitness and propriety in making suffering the accompaniment of vice, quite apart from any benefit

"POLITICAL JUSTICE"

that may be in the result. No adherent of the doctrine of necessity in morals can justify that attitude. The assassin could no more avoid the murder he committed than could the dagger. Justice opposes any suffering which is not attended by benefit. Resentment against vice will not excuse useless torture. We must banish the conception of desert. To punish for what is past and irrecoverable must be ranked among the most baleful conceptions of barbarism. Xerxes was not more unreasonable when he lashed the waves of the sea, than that man would be who inflicted suffering on his fellow from a view to the past and not from a view to the future.

Excluding all idea of punishment in the proper sense of the word, it remains only to consider such coercion as is used against persons convicted of injurious action in the past, for the purpose of preventing future mischief. Godwin now invites us to consider the futility of coercion as a means of reforming, or as he would say, " enlightening the understanding " of a man who has erred. Our aim is to bring him to the acceptance of our conception of duty. Assuming that we possess more of eternal justice than he, do we shrink from setting our wit against his? Instead of acting as his preceptor we become his tyrant. Coercion first annihilates the understanding of its victim, and then of him who adopts it. Dressed in the supine prerogatives of a master, he is excused from cultivating the faculties of a man. Coercion begins by producing pain, by violently alienating the mind from the truth with which we wish it to be impressed. It includes a tacit confession of imbecility.

With some hesitation Godwin allows the use of force to restrain a man found in actual violence. We may not have time to reason with him. But even for self-defence there are other resources. " The powers of the mind are yet unfathomed." He tells the story of Marius, who overawed the soldier sent into his cell to execute him, with the words, " Wretch, have you the temerity to kill Marius ? " Were we all accustomed to place an intrepid confidence in the unaided energy of the intellect, to despise force in others and to refuse to employ it ourselves, who shall say how far the species might be improved ? But punitive coercion deals only with a man whose violence is over. The only rational excuse for it is to restrain a man from further violence which he will presumably commit. **Godwin** condemns capital punishment as

"POLITICAL JUSTICE" 129

excessive, since restraint can be attained without it, and corporal chastisement as an offence against the dignity of the human mind. Let there be nothing in the state of transition worse than simple imprisonment. Godwin, however, dissents vehemently from Howard's invention of solitary confinement, designed to shield the prisoner from the contamination of his fellow criminals. Man is a social animal and virtue depends on social relations. As a preliminary to acquiring it is he to be shut out from the society of his fellows ? How shall he exercise benevolence or justice in his cell ? Will his heart become softened or expand who breathes the atmosphere of a dungeon ? Solitary confinement is the bitterest torment that human ingenuity can inflict. The least objectionable method of depriving a criminal of the power to harm society is banishment or transportation. Expose him to the stimulus of necessity in an unsettled country. New conditions make new minds. But the whole attempt to apply law breaks down. You must heap edict on edict, and to make your laws fit your cases, must either for ever wrest them or make new ones. Law does not end uncertainty, and it debilitates the mind. So long as men are habituated to look to foreign guidance and external rules for direction, so long the vigour of their minds will sleep.

If Fénelon, saint and philosopher, with an incompleted masterpiece in his pocket, and Fénelon's chambermaid, were both in danger of burning to death in the archiepiscopal palace at Cambrai, and if I could save only one of them, which ought I to save? It is a fascinating problem in casuistry, and Godwin with his usual decision of mind, has no doubt about the solution. He would save Fénelon as the more valuable life, and above all Fénelon's manuscript, and the maid, he is quite sure, would wish to give her life for his. Something (the modern reader will object) might be urged on the other side. Just because he was a saint, it might be argued that he was the fitter of the two to face the great adventure, and one may be sure that he himself would have thought so. A philosopher who gives his life for a kitten will have advanced the Kingdom of Heaven. The chambermaid, moreover, may have in her a potentiality of love and happiness which are worth many a masterpiece of French prose. But Godwin has not yet exhausted his moral problem. How, if the maid were my mother, wife or benefactress? Once more he gives his unflinching answer. Justice still requires of me in the interests of mankind to save the more valuable life. "What magic is there in the pronoun 'my' to overturn the decisions of everlasting truth?" My mother may be a fool, a liar, or a thief. Of what consequence then, is it that she is "mine"? Gratitude ought not to blind me to my duty, though she have suckled me and nursed me. The benevolence of a benefactor ought indeed to be esteemed, but not because it benefited me. A benefactor ought to be esteemed as much by another as by me, solely because he benefited a human being. Gratitude, in short, has no place in justice or virtue, and reason declines to recognise the private affections.

Such, crudely stated, is Godwin's famous doctrine of "universal benevolence." The virtuous man is like Swift's Houyhnhnms, noble quadrupeds, wholly governed by reason, who cared for strangers as well as for the nearest neighbour, and showed the same affection for their neighbour's offspring as for their own. The centre of Godwin's moral teaching was yet another Socratic thought. Politics are "the proper vehicle of a liberal morality," and morals concern our relation to the whole body of mankind. To realise justice is our prime concern as rational beings, and society is nothing but embodied justice. Justice deals with beings capable of pleasure and pain. Here we are partakers of a common nature with like faculties for suffering or enjoyment. " Justice," then, " is that impartial treatment of every man in matters that relate to his happiness, which is measured solely by a consideration of the properties of the receiver and the capacity of him who gives." Every man with whom I am in contact is a sentient being, and one should be as much to me as another, save indeed where equity corrects equality, by suggesting to me that one individual may be of more value than another, because of his greater power to benefit mankind. Justice exacts from us the application of our talents, time, and resources with the single object of producing the greatest sum of benefit to sentient beings. There is no limit to what I am bound to do for the general weal. I hold my person and property both in trust on behalf of mankind. A man who needs £10 has an absolute claim on me, if I have it, unless it can be shown that the money could be more beneficially applied. Every shilling I possess is irrevocably assigned by some claim of eternal justice. Every article of property, it follows, should

"POLITICAL JUSTICE" 133

belong to him in whose hands it will be of most benefit, and the instrument of the greatest happiness.

It is the love of distinction which attends wealth in corrupt societies that explains the desire for luxury. We desire not the direct pleasure to be derived from excessive possessions, but the consideration which is attached to it. Our very clothes are an appeal to the goodwill of our neighbours, and a refuge from their contempt. Society would be transformed if the distinction were reversed, if admiration were no longer rendered to the luxurious and avaricious and were accorded only to talent and virtue. Let not the necessity of rewarding virtue be suggested as a justification for the inequalities of fortune. Shall we say, to a virtuous man : " If you show yourself deserving, you shall have the essence of a hundred times more food than you can eat, and a hundred times more clothes than you can wear. You shall have a patent for taking away from others the means f a happy and respectable existence, and for consuming them in riotous and unmeaning extravagance." Is this the reward that ought to be offered to virtue, or that virtue should stoop to take ? Godwin is at his best on this theme of luxury : " Every man may calculate in every glass of wine he drinks, and every ornament he annexes to his person, how many individuals have been condemned to slavery and sweat, incessant drudgery, unwholesome food, continual hardships, deplorable ignorance and brutal insensibility, that he may be supplied with these luxuries. It is a gross imposition that men are accustomed to put upon themselves, when they talk of the property bequeathed to them by their ancestors. The property is produced by the daily labour of men who are now in existence. All that the ancestors bequeathed to them was a mouldy patent which they show as a title to extort from their neighbours what the labour of those neighbours has produced."

It is a flagrant immorality that one man should have the power to dispose of the produce of another man's toil, yet to maintain this power is the main concern of police and legislation. Morality recognises two degrees of property, (1) things which will produce the greatest benefit, if attributed to me, in brief the necessities of life, my food, clothes, furniture and apartment ; (2) the empire which every man may claim over the produce of his own industry, even over that part of it which ought not to be used and appropriated

"POLITICAL JUSTICE"

by himself. Every man is a steward. But subject to censure and remonstrance, he must be free to dispose of his property as his own understanding shall dictate. The ideal is equality, and all society should be what Coleridge called a Pantisocracy. It is wrong for any one to enjoy anything, unless something similar is accessible to all, and wrong to produce luxuries until the elementary wants of all are satisfied. But it would be futile and wrong to attempt to equalise property by positive enactment. It would be useless until men are virtuous, and unnecessary when they are so. The moment accumulation and monopoly are regarded by any society as dishonourable and mischievous, the revolution in opinion will ensure that comforts shall tend to a level.

Godwin objects to the plans put forward in France during the Revolution for interfering with bequests and inheritance. He would, however, check the incentives to accumulation by abolishing the feudal system, primogeniture, titles and entail. Property is sacred —that good men may be free to give it away. Reform public opinion, and a man engaged in amassing wealth would soon hide his treasures as carefully as he now displays them. The first step is to rob wealth of its distinction.

Wealth is acquired to-day in over-reaching our neighbours, and spent in insulting them. Establish equality on a firm basis of rational opinion, and you cut off for ever the great occasion of crime, remove the constant spectacle of injustice with all its attendant demoralisation, and liberate genius now immersed in sordid cares.

"In a state of society where men lived in the midst of plenty, and where all shared alike the bounties of nature, the sentiments of oppression, servility and fraud would inevitably expire. The narrow principle of selfishness would vanish. No man being obliged to guard his little store, or provide with anxiety and pain for his restless wants, each would lose his individual existence in the thought of the general good. No man would be an enemy to his neighbour, for they would have no subject of contention, and of consequence philanthropy would resume the empire which reason assigns her. Mind would be delivered from her perpetual anxiety about corporal support, and freed to expatiate in the field of thought, which is congenial to her. Each would assist the enquiries of all."

Unnecessary tasks absorb most of our labour to-day. In the ideal community,

"POLITICAL JUSTICE"

Godwin reckons that half an hour's toil from every man daily will suffice to produce the necessities of life. He modified this sanguine estimate in a later essay (*The Enquirer*) to two hours. He dismisses all objections based on the sloth or selfishness of human nature, by the simple answer that this happy state of things will not be realised until human nature has been reformed. Need individuality suffer? It need fear only the restraint imposed by candid public opinion. That will not be irksome, because it will be frank. We shrink from it to-day, only because it takes the form of clandestine scandal and backbiting. Godwin contemplates no Spartan plan of common labour or common meals. " Everything understood by the term co-operation is in some sense an evil." To be sure, it may be indispensable in order to cut a canal or navigate a ship. But mechanical invention will gradually make it unnecessary. The Spartans used slaves. We shall make machines our helots. Indeed, so odious is co-operation to a free mind, that Godwin marvels that men can consent to play music in concert, or can demean themselves to execute another man's compositions, while to act a part in a play amounts almost to an offence against sincerity. Such extravagances as this passage are amongst the most precious things in *Political Justice*. Godwin was a fanatic of logic who warns us against his individualist premises by pressing them to a fantastic conclusion.

The sketch of the ideal community concludes with a demolition of the family. Cohabitation, he argued, is in itself an evil. It melts opinions to a common mould, and destroys the fortitude of the individual. The wishes of two people who live together can never wholly coincide. Hence follow thwartings of the will, bickering and misery. No man is always cheerful and kind. We manage to correct a stranger with urbanity and good humour. Only when the intercourse is too close and unremitted do we degenerate into surliness and invective. In an earlier chapter Godwin had formulated a general objection to all promises, which reminds us of Tolstoy's sermons from the same individualistic standpoint on the text, " Swear not at all." Every conceivable mode of action has its tendency to benefit or injure mankind. I am bound in duty to one course of action in every emergency—the course most conducive to the general welfare. Why, then, should I bind myself by a promise ? If my promise contradicts my duty it is immoral,

"POLITICAL JUSTICE" 139

if it agrees with it, it teaches me to do that from a precarious and temporary motive which ought to be done from its intrinsic recommendations. By promising we bind ourselves to learn nothing from time, to make no use of knowledge to be acquired. Promises depose us from a full use of our understanding, and are to be tolerated only in the trivial engagements of our day-to-day existence. It follows that marriage is an evil, for it is at once the closest form of cohabitation, and the rashest of all promises. Two thoughtless and romantic people, met in youth under circumstances full of delusion, have bound themselves, not by reason but by contract, to make the best, when they discover their deception, of an irretrievable mistake. Its maxim is, "If you have made a mistake, cherish it." So long as this institution survives, "philanthropy will be crossed in a thousand ways, and the still augmenting stream of abuse continue to flow."

Godwin has little fear of lust or license. Men will, on the whole, continue to prefer one partner, and friendship will refine the grossness of sense. There are worse evils than open and avowed inconstancy—the loathsome combination of deceitful intrigue with the selfish monopoly of property. That a child should know its father is no great matter, for I ought not in reason to prefer one human being to another because he is "mine." The mother will care for the child with the spontaneous help of her neighbours. As to the business of supplying children with food and clothing, "these would easily find their true level and spontaneously flow from the quarter in which they abounded to the quarter that was deficient." There must be no barter or exchange, but only giving from pure benevolence without the prospect of reciprocal advantage.

The picture of this easy-going Utopia, in which something will always turn up for nobody's child, concludes with two sections which exhibit in nice juxtaposition the extravagance and the prudence of Godwin. We may look forward to great physical changes. We shall acquire an empire over our bodies, and may succeed in making even our reflex notions conscious. We must get rid of sleep, one of the most conspicuous infirmities of the human frame. Life can be prolonged by intellect. We are sick and we die because in a certain sense we consent to suffer these accidents. When the limit of population is reached, men will refuse to propagate themselves further. Society will be a people of men, and not of children, adult, veteran, experienced; and truth will no longer have to recommence her career at the end of thirty years. Meanwhile let the friends of justice avoid violence, eschew massacres, and remember that prudent handling will win even rich men for the cause of human perfection.

So ends *Political Justice*, the strangest amalgam in our literature of caution with enthusiasm, of visions with experience, of French logic with English tactlessness, a book which only genius could have made so foolish and so wise.

CHAPTER V

GODWIN AND THE REACTION

Political Justice brought its author instant fame. Society was for a moment intimidated by the boldness of the attack. The world was in a generous mood, and men did not yet resent Godwin's flattering suggestion that they were demigods who disguised their own greatness. He had assailed all the accepted dogmas and venerable institutions of contemporary civilisation, from monarchy to marriage, but it was only after several years that society recovered its breath, and turned to rend him. He became an oracle in an ever-widening circle of friends, and was naïvely pleased to find, when he went into the country, that even in remote villages his name was known. He was everywhere received as a sage, and some years passed before he discovered how much of this deference was a polite disguise for the vulgar curiosity that attends a sudden celebrity. Prosperity was a wholesome stimulus. He was " exalted in spirits," and became for a time (he tells us) "more of a talker than I was before, or have been since."

In this mood he wrote the one book which has lived as a popular possession, and held its place among the classics which are frequently reprinted. *Caleb Williams* (published in 1794) is incomparably the best of his novels, and the one great work of fiction in our language which owes its existence to the fruitful union of the revolutionary and romantic movements. It spoke to its own day as Hugo's *Les Misérables* and Tolstoy's *Resurrection* spoke to later generations. It is as its preface tells us, " a general review of the modes of domestic and unrecorded despotism by which man becomes the destroyer of man." It conveys in the form of an eventful personal history the essence of the criticism against society, which had inspired *Political Justice.* Godwin's imagination was haunted by a persistent nightmare, in which a lonely individual finds arrayed against him all the prejudices of society, all the forms of convention, all the forces of law. They hurl themselves upon him in a pitiless pursuit, and wherever he flees, the pervading corruptions, the ingrained cowardices of over-governed mankind beset his feet like gins and pitfalls. It was a hereditary nightmare, and with a less pedestrian imagination, his daughter, Mary Shelley, used the same theme of a remorseless pursuit in *Frankenstein*.

Caleb Williams, a promising lad of humble birth but good parts, is broken at the outset of his career, in the tremendous clash between two formidable characters, who represent, each in his own way, the corruptions of aristocracy. Mr. Tyrrel is a brutal English squire, a coarse and domineering bully, whom birth and wealth arm with the power to crush his dependents. Mr. Falkland personifies the spirit of chivalry at its best and its worst. All his native humanity and acquired polish is in the end turned to cruelty by the influence of a worship of honour and reputation which make him " the fool of fame." As the absorbing story unfolds itself, we realise (if indeed we are not too much enthralled by the plot to notice the moral) that all the institutions of society and law are nicely adjusted to give the moral errors of the great their utmost scope. Society is a vast sounding-board which echoes the first whispers of their private folly, until it swells into a deafening chorus of cruelty and wrong. There are vivid scenes in a prison which give life to Godwin's reasoned criticisms of our penal methods. There is a

GODWIN AND THE REACTION 145

band of outlaws whose rude natural virtues remind us, by contrast with the corruption of all the officers of the law, how much less demoralising it is to revolt against a crazy system of coercion than to become its tool. To describe the book in greater detail would be to destroy the pleasure of the reader. It is a forensic novel. It sets out to frame an indictment of society, and a novelist who imposes this task on himself must in the end create an impression of improbability by the partiality with which he selects his material. But there is fire enough in the telling, and interest enough in the plot to silence our criticisms while we read. *Caleb Williams* is a capital story; it is also a living and humane book, which conveys with rare power and reasoned emotion the revolt of a generous mind against the oppressions of feudalism and the stupidities of the criminal law.

Three years later (1797) Godwin once more restated the main positions of *Political Justice*. *The Enquirer* is a volume of essays, which range easily over a great variety of subjects from education to English style. His opinions have neither advanced nor receded, and the mood is still one of assurance, enthusiasm, and hope. The only noteworthy change is in the style. *Political Justice* belongs to the generation of Gibbon, eloquent, elaborate and periodic at its best; heavy and slightly verbose at its worst. With *The Enquirer* we are just entering the generation of Hazlitt and Leigh Hunt. The language is simpler and more flexible, the construction of the sentences more varied, the mood more vivacious, and the tone more conversational. The best things in the book belong to that social psychology, the observation of men in classes and professions, in which this age excelled. There is an outspoken attack on the clergy, as a class of men who have vowed themselves to study without enquiry, who must reason for ever towards a conclusion fixed by authority, whose very survival depends on the perennial stationariness of their understanding. Another essay attempts a vivacious criticism of " common honesty," the moral standard of the average decent citizen, a code of negative virtues and moral mediocrity which is content to avoid the obvious unsocial sins and concerns itself but little to enforce positive benevolence. The reader who would meet Godwin at his best should turn to the essay *On Servants*. Starting from the universal reluctance of the upper and middle classes to allow their children to associate closely with servants, he enlarges the confession of the systematic degradation of a class which this separation involves, into a condemnation of our whole social structure.

The year 1797 marks the culmination of Godwin's career, and it would have been well for his fame if it had been its end. He had just passed his fortieth year; he had made the most notable contribution to English political thought since the appearance of the *Wealth of Nations*; he had won the gratitude and respect of his friends by his intervention in the trial of the Twelve Reformers. He was famous, prosperous, popular, and his good fortune brought to his calm temperament the stimulus of excitement and high spirits which it needed. There came to him in this year the crown of a noble love. It was in the winter of 1791 that he first met Mary Wollstonecraft, the one woman of genius who belonged to the English revolutionary circle. He was not impressed, thought that she talked too much, and in his diary spelled her name incorrectly.

In the interval between 1791 and 1797 Mary Wollstonecraft was to write one of the books which belong to the spiritual foundations of the next century, to taste fame and detraction, to know the joys of love and maternity, and to experience a misery and wrong which made life itself an unendurable shame. A later chapter will attempt an estimate of the ideas and personality of this brilliant and courageous woman. A few sentences must suffice here to recall the bare facts of her life history. Born in 1759, the child of a drunken and disreputable father, she had struggled with indomitable energy, first as a teacher and then as a translator and literary " hack," to keep herself and help her still more unfortunate sisters. In 1792 she published *A Vindication of the Rights of Woman,* a plea for the human dignity of her sex and for its claim to education. At the end of this year she went to Paris as much to see the Revolution as to perfect herself in French. She there met a clever and interesting American, one Gilbert Imlay, a traveller of some little note, a soldier in the War of Independence, and now a speculative merchant. He lived with her, and in documents acknowledged her as his wife, though neither felt the need of a binding ceremony. A baby, Fanny, was born, but Imlay's business imposed long separations. He gradually tired of the woman who had honoured him too highly, and entered on

GODWIN AND THE REACTION

more than one intrigue. Mary Wollstonecraft attempted in despair to drown herself in the Thames, was saved and nursed back to life and courage by devoted friends. She again took up her pen to gain a livelihood, and for the sake of her child's future, gradually returned to the literary circle which valued her, not merely for her genius and originality, but also for her beauty, her vivacity, and her charm, for her daring and independence, and her warm, impulsive, affectionate heart.

Godwin met her again while she was bruised and lonely and disillusionised with mankind. Her charming volume of travel sketches (*Letters from Norway*, 1796) had made, as it well might, a deep impression on his taste. He was, what Imlay was not, her intellectual equal, and his character deserved her respect. He has left in the little book which he published to vindicate her memory, a delicate sketch of their mutual love : " The partiality we conceived for each other was in that mode which I have always considered as the purest and most refined style of love. It grew with equal advances in the mind of each. It would have been impossible for the most minute observer to have said who was before and who was after. One sex did not take the priority which long-established custom has awarded it, nor the other overstep that delicacy which is so severely imposed. I am not conscious that either party can assume to have been the agent or the patient, the toil spreader or the prey in the affair. When in the course of things, the disclosure came, there was nothing in a manner for either party to disclose to the other. . . . There was no period of throes and resolute explanation attendant on the tale. It was friendship melting into love."

The two lovers, in strict obedience to the principles of *Political Justice*, made their home, at first with no legal union, in a little house in the Polygon, Somers Town, then the extreme limit of London, separated from the suburban village of Camden Town by open fields and green pastures. A few doors away Godwin had his study, where he spent most of his industrious day, often breakfasted and sometimes slept. Both partners of this daringly unconventional union had their own particular friends and retained their separate places in society. Some quaint notes have survived, which passed between them, borrowing books or making appointments. " Did I not see you, friend Godwin," runs one of these, " at the theatre last night ?

GODWIN AND THE REACTION 151

I thought I met a smile, but you went out without looking round. We expect you at half-past four." It was the coming of a child which induced them to waive their theories and face for its sake a repugnant compliance with custom. They were married in Old St. Pancras Church on March 29, 1797, and the insignificant fact was communicated only gradually, and with laboured apologies for the inconsistency, to their friends.

Southey, who met them in this month, has left a lively portrait: "Of all the lions or literati I have seen here, Mary Imlay's countenance is the best, infinitely the best: the only fault in it is an expression somewhat similar to what the prints of Horne Tooke display—an expression indicating superiority; not haughtiness, not sarcasm in Mary Imlay, but still it is unpleasant. Her eyes are light brown, and . . . they are the most meaning I ever saw. . . As for Godwin himself he has large noble eyes and a *nose* —oh, most abominable nose. Language is not vituperatious enough to describe the effect of its downward elongation." Godwin, if one may trust the portrait by Northcote, had impressive if not exactly handsome features. The head is shapely, the brow ample, the nose decidedly too long, the shaven lips and chin finely chiselled. The whole suggestion is of a character self-absorbed and contemplative. He was short and sturdy in build, and in his sober dress and grave deportments, suggested rather the dissenting preacher than the prophet of philosophic anarchism. He was not a ready debater or a fluent talker. His genius was not spontaneous or intuitive. It was rather an elaborate effort of the will, which deliberately used the fruits of his accumulative study and incessant activity of mind. He resembled, says Hazlitt, who admired and liked him, " an eight-day clock that must be wound up long before it can strike. He is ready only on reflection: dangerous only at the rebound. He gathers himself up, and strains every nerve and faculty with deliberate aim to some heroic and dazzling achievement of intellect; but he must make a career before he flings himself armed upon the enemy, or he is sure to be unhorsed."

No two minds could have presented a greater contrast. Had Mary Wollstonecraft lived they must have moulded each other into something finer than Nature had made of either. The year of married life was ideally happy, and the strange experiment in reconciling individualism with love apparently suc-

GODWIN AND THE REACTION 153

ceeded. Mrs. Godwin, for all her revolutionary independence, leaned affectionately on her husband, and he, in spite of his rather overgrown self-esteem, regarded her with reverence and pride. She was quick in her affections and resentments, but looking back many years later Godwin declares that they were " as happy as is permitted to human beings." " It must be remembered, however, that I honoured her intellectual powers and the nobleness and generosity of her propensities; mere tenderness would not have been adequate to produce the happiness we experienced."

Godwin's novels suggest that, on the whole, he shared her views about women, though in a later essay (on " Friendship," in *Thoughts on Man*), there are some passages which suggest a less perfect understanding. But he never used his pen to carry on her work, and the emancipation of women had to await its philosopher in John Stuart Mill. The happy marriage ended abruptly and tragically. On August 30, 1797, was born the child Mary, who was to become Shelley's wife, and carry on in a second generation her parents' tradition of fearless love and revolutionary hope. Ten days after the birth, the mother died in spite of all that the devotion of her husband and the skill of his medical friends could do to save her. A few broken-hearted letters are left to record Godwin's agony of mind.

With the death of Mary Wollstonecraft in 1797, ended all that was happy and stimulating in Godwin's career. It was for him the year of private disaster, and from it he dated also the triumph of the reaction in England. The stimulus of the revolutionary period was withdrawn. He lived no longer among ardent spirits who would brave everything and do anything for human perfectibility. Some were in Botany Bay, and others, like the indomitable Holcroft, were absorbed in the struggle to live, with the handicap of political persecution against them. Godwin, indeed, never fell into despair over the ruin of his political hopes. Like Beethoven he revered Napoleon, at all events until he assumed the title of Emperor, and would console himself with the conviction that this "auspicious and beneficent genius" had "without violence to the principles of the French Revolution . . . suspended their morbid activity," while preserving "all the great points" of its doctrine. But while all England hung on the event of the titanic

GODWIN AND THE REACTION 155

struggle against this "beneficent genius," what was a philanthropist to do? The world was rattling back into barbarism, and the generation which emerged from the long nightmare of war, famine, and repression, was incomparably less advanced in its thinking, narrower and timider in its whole habit of mind than the men who were young in 1789. There was nothing to do, and a philosopher whose only weapon was argument, kept silence when none would listen. Of what use to talk of "peace and the powers of the human mind," while all England was gloating over the brutal cartoons of Gillray, and trying on the volunteer uniforms, in which it hoped to repel Napoleon's invasion? We need not wonder that Godwin's output of philosophic writing practically ceased with the eighteenth century. He was henceforth a man without a purpose, who wrote for bread and renounced the exercise of his greater powers.

The end of Godwin's active apostolic life is clearly marked in a pamphlet which he issued in 1801 ("Thoughts occasioned by the Perusal of Dr. Parr's Spital Sermon, preached at Christ Church, April 15, 1800, being a reply to the attacks of Dr. Parr, Mr. Mackintosh, the author [Malthus] of the *Essay on*

Population and others "). It is a masterly piece of writing. Coleridge scribbled in the copy that now lies on the shelves of the British Museum this tribute to its author: " I remember few passages in ancient or modern authors that contain more just philosophy in appropriate, chaste or beautiful diction than the fine following pages. They reflect equal honour on Godwin's head and heart. Though I did it in the zenith of his reputation, yet I feel remorse even to have only spoken unkindly of such a man.—S. T. C."

Godwin tells how the reaction burst over him, and he dates it from 1797 : " After having for four years heard little else than the voice of commendation, I was at length attacked from every side, and in a style which defied all moderation and decency. . . . The cry spread like a general infection, and I have been told that not even a petty novel for boarding-school misses now ventures to aspire to favour unless it contains some expression of dislike or abhorrence to the new philosophy." Some of the attacks were scurrilous and all of them proceeded on the common assumption of the defenders of authority in all ages and nations, that the man who would innovate in morals is himself immoral.

GODWIN AND THE REACTION

He goes on to sketch the present case of the revolutionary party: "The societies have perished, or where they have not, have shrunk to a skeleton; the days of democratical declamation are no more; even the starving labourer in the alehouse is become the champion of aristocracy. . . . Jacobinism was destroyed; its party as a party was extinguished; its tenets were involved in almost universal unpopularity and odium; they were deserted by almost every man high or low in the island of Great Britain." Even the young Pantisocrats had gone over to the enemy, and Wordsworth, grave and disillusioned, tried to forget that he had ever exhorted his fellow-students to burn their books and "read Godwin on Necessity." The defection of Dr. Parr and Mackintosh was symptomatic. Both had been Godwin's personal friends, and both of them had hailed the new philosophy. No one remembers them to-day, but they were in their time intellectual oracles. The scholar Parr was called by flatterers the Whig Johnson, and Mackintosh enjoyed in Whig society a reputation as a brilliant talker, and an encyclopædic mind which reminds us of Macaulay's later fame. They had both to make their peace with the world and to bury their compromised past; the easiest way was to fall upon Godwin.

Malthus was a more worthy antagonist, though Godwin did not yet perceive how formidable his attack in reality was. To the picture of human perfection he opposed the nightmare of an over-populated planet, and combated universal benevolence by teaching that even charity is an economic sin. English society cares little either for Utopias or for science. But it welcomes science with rapture when it destroys Utopias. If Godwin had pricked men's consciences, Malthus brought the balm. Altruism was exposed at length for the thing it was, an error in the last degree unscientific and uneconomic. The rickety arithmetic of Malthusianism was used against the revolutionary hope, exactly as a travestied version of Darwinianism was used in our own day against Socialism. Godwin preserved his dignity in this controversy and made concessions to his critics with a rare candour. But while he abandons none of his fundamental doctrines, one feels that he will never fight again.

Only once in later years did Godwin the philosopher break his silence, and then it was to attempt in 1820 an elaborate but far from impressive answer to Malthus. The

GODWIN AND THE REACTION 159

history of that controversy has been brilliantly told by Hazlitt. It seems to-day too distant to be worth reviving. Our modern pessimists write their jeremiads not about the future over-population of the planet, but about the declining birth-rate. That elaborate civilisations shows a decline in fertility is a fact now so well recognised, that we feel no difficulty in conceding to Godwin that the reasonable beings of his ideal community might be trusted to show some degree of self-control.

Godwin possessed two of the cardinal virtues of a thinker, courage and candour. No fear of ridicule deterred him from pushing his premises to their last conclusion; no false shame restrained him in a controversy from recanting an error. He discarded the wilder developments of his theory of "universal benevolence," and gave it in the end a form which has ceased to be paradoxical. When he wrote *Political Justice* he was a celibate student who had escaped much of the formative experience of a normal life. As a husband and a father he revised his creed, and devoted no small part of his later literary activity to the work of preaching the claims of those "private affections" which he had scouted as an elderly youth of forty. The re-adjustment in his theory was so simple, that only a great philosopher could have failed to make it sooner. Justice requires me to use all my powers to contribute to the sum of human benefit. But as regards opportunity, I am not equally situated towards all my fellows. By devoting myself more particularly to wife or child with an exclusive affection which is not in the abstract altogether reasonable, I may do more for the general good than I could achieve by a severely impartial benevolence.

He developed this view first in his *Memoir of Mary Wollstonecraft*, then in the preface to *St. Leon*, and finally in the pamphlet which answered Mackintosh and Dr. Parr. The man who would be " the best moral economist of his time " will use much of it to seek " the advantage and content of those with whom he has most frequent intercourse," and this not merely from calculation, but from affection. " I ought not only in ordinary cases to provide for my wife and children, my brothers and relations before I provide for strangers, but it would be well that my doing so should arise from the operation of those private and domestic affections by which through all ages of the world the conduct of mankind has been excited and directed."

The recantation is sufficiently frank. The

GODWIN AND THE REACTION

family, dissipated in *Political Justice* by the explosive charities of "universal benevolence," is now happily re-united. Godwin maintains, however, that his moral theory and his political superstructure stands intact, and the claim is not unreasonable. He retains his criterion of justice and utility, though he has seen better how to apply it. The duty of universal benevolence is still paramount; the end of contributing to the general good still sovereign, and a reasoned virtue is still to be recommended in preference to instinctive goodness, even where their results are commonly the same. "The crown of a virtuous character consists in a very frequent and very energetic recollection of the criterion by which all his actions are to be tried. . . . The person who has been well instructed and accomplished in the great schools of human experience has passions and affections like other men. But he is aware that all these affections tend to excess, and must be taught each to know its order and its sphere. He therefore continually holds in mind the principles by which their boundaries are fixed."

What Godwin means is something elementary, and for that reason of the first importance. Let a man love his wife above other women, but "universal benevolence" will forbid him to exploit other women in order to surround her with luxury. Let him love his sons, but virtue will forbid him to accumulate a fortune for them by the sweated labour of poor men's children. Let him love his fellow-countrymen, but reason forbids him to seek their good by enslaving other races and waging aggressive wars. Godwin, in short, no longer denies the beauty and duty (to use Burke's phrase) of loving " the little platoon to which I belong," but he urges that these domestic affections are in little danger of neglect. Men learned to love kith and kin, neighbours and comrades, while still in the savage state. The characteristic of a civilised morality, the necessary accompaniment of all the varied and extended relationships which modern existence has brought with it, must be a new and emphatic stress on my duty to the stranger, to the unknown producer with whom I stand in an economic relationship, and to the foreigner beyond my shores. "Let us endeavour to elevate philanthropy into a passion, secure that occasions enough will arise to drag us down from an enthusiastic eminence. A virtuous man will teach himself to recollect the principle of universal benevolence as often as pious men repeat their prayers."

GODWIN AND THE REACTION

If the central tendencies of Godwin's teaching survive these later modifications, it is none the less true that some of his theoretic foundations have been shaken in the work of reconstruction. The isolated individual shut up in his own animal skin and communicating with his fellows through the antennæ of his logical processes, has vanished away. Allow him to extend his personality through the private affections, and he has ceased to be the abstract unit of individualism. Godwin should have revised not only his doctrine of the family, but his hatred of co-operation. There is still something to be learned from the view of his school that the human mind, as it begins to absorb the collective experience of the race, is an infinitely variable spiritual stuff, an intellectual protoplasm. They stated the view with a rash emphasis, until one is forced to ask whether a mind which is originally nothing at all, can absorb, or as psychologists say, " apperceive " anything whatever. Nothing comes out of nothing, and nothing can be added to nothing.

Godwin and his school set out to show that the human mind is not necessarily fettered for all time by the prejudices and institutions in which it has clothed itself. When he had done stripping us, it was a nice question whether even our nakedness remained. He treated our prejudices and our effete institutions as though they were something external to us, which had come out of nowhere and could be flung into the void from whence they came. When you have called opinion a prejudice, or traced an institution to false reasoning, you have, after all, only exhibited an interesting zoological fact about human beings. We are exactly the sort of creature which evolves such prejudices. Godwin in unwary moments would talk as though aristocracy and positive law had come to us from without, by a sort of diabolic revelation. This, however, is not a criticism which destroys the value of his thinking. His positions required restatement in terms of the idea of development. If he did not anticipate the notion of evolution, he was the apostle of the idea of progress. We may still retain from his reasonings the hopeful conclusion that the human mind is a raw material capable of almost unlimited variation, and, therefore, of some advance towards " perfection." We owe an inestimable debt to the school which proclaimed this belief in enthusiastic paradoxes.

Godwin's influence as a thinker permeated the older generation of " philosophic radicals " in England. The oddest fact about it is that it had apparently no part in founding the later philosophic anarchism of the Continent. None of its leaders seem to have read him; and *Political Justice* was not translated into German until long after it had ceased to be read in England. Its really astonishing blindness to the importance of the economic factor in social changes must have hastened its decline. Godwin writes as though he had never seen a factory nor heard of capital. In all his writing about crime and punishment, full as it is of insight, sympathy and good sense, it is odd that a mind so fertile nowhere anticipated the modern doctrine of the connection between moral and physical degeneracy. He saw in crime only error, where we see anæmia: he would have cured it with syllogisms, where we should administer proteids. His entire psychology, both social and individual, is vitiated by a naïve and headstrong intellectualism. Life is rather a battle between narrow interests and the social affections than a debate between sound and fallacious reasoning. He saw among mankind only sophists and philosophers, where we see predatory egoists and their starved and stunted victims. But we have advanced far enough on our own lines of thinking to derive a new stimulus from Godwin's one-sided intellectualism. Our danger to-day is that we may succumb to an economic and physiological determinism. We are obsessed by financiers and bacilli; it is salutary that our attention should be directed from time to time to the older bogeys of the revolution, to kings and priests, authority and superstition, to prejudice and political subjection. " The greatest part of the people of Europe," wrote Helvétius, " honour virtue in speculation; this is an effect of their education. They despise it in practice; that is an effect of the form of their governments." We think that we have got beyond that epigram to-day. But have we quite exhausted its meaning?

Precisely because of its revolutionary *naïveté*, its unscientific innocence, there is in Godwin's democratic anarchism a stimulus peculiarly tonic to the modern mind. No man has developed more firmly the ideal of universal enlightenment, which has escaped feudalism, only to be threatened by the sociological expert. No writer is better fitted to remind us that society and government are not the same thing, and that the State must not be confounded with the social organism. No moralist has written a more eloquent page on the evil of coercion and the unreason of

GODWIN AND THE REACTION

force. *Political Justice* is often an imposing system. It is sometimes an instructive fallacy. It is always an inspiring sermon. Godwin hoped to " make it a work from the perusal of which no man should rise without being strengthened in habits of sincerity, fortitude and justice." There he succeeded.

CHAPTER VI

GODWIN AND SHELLEY

In a letter written in 1811 Shelley records how he suddenly heard with " inconceivable emotion " that Godwin was still alive. He " had enrolled his name on the list of the honourable dead." Godwin, to quote Hazlitt's rather cruel phrase, had " sunk below the horizon," in his later years, and enjoyed " the serene twilight of a doubtful immortality." Serene unfortunately it was not. With a lonely home and two little girls to care for, Godwin thought once more of marriage. Twice his wooing was unsuccessful, and the philosopher who believed that reason was omnipotent, tried in vain in long, elaborate letters to argue two ladies into love. His second wife came unsought. As he sat one day at his window in the Polygon, a handsome widow spoke to him from the neighbouring balcony, with these arresting words, " Is it possible that I behold the immortal Godwin ? " They were married before the close of the year (1801).

GODWIN AND SHELLEY 169

Mrs. Clairmont was a strange successor to Mary Wollstonecraft. She was a vulgar and worldly woman, thoroughly feminine, and rather inclined to boast of her total ignorance of philosophy. A kindly and loyal wife she may have been, but she was jealous of Godwin's friends, and would tell petty lies to keep them apart from him. She brought with her two children of a former marriage— Charles (who was unhappy in this strange home and went early abroad) and Jane. On this clever, pretty and mercurial daughter all her partiality was lavished; and the unhappy girl, pampered by a philistine mother in a revolutionary atmosphere, was at the age of seventeen seduced by Byron, and became the mother of the fairy child, Allegra. The second Mrs. Godwin was the stepmother of convention, and treated both Fanny Imlay and Mary Godwin with consistent unkindness. It was the fate of the gentle, melancholy and lovable Fanny to take her own life at the age of twenty-two (1816). The destiny of these children, all gifted with what the age called sensibility, has served as the text of many a sermon against "the new philosophy." No one, however, can read the documents which this strange household left behind, without feeling that the parent of the disaster in their lives was not their philosophic father, but this commonplace " womanly woman," who flattered, intrigued, and lied. In 1803, there was born of this second marriage, a son, William, who inherited something of his father's ability. He became a journalist, and died at the early age of twenty-nine, after publishing a novel of some promise, *Transfusion*, steeped in the same romantic fancies which colour Mary Shelley's more famous *Frankenstein*.

With the cares of this family on his shoulders Godwin began to form the habit of applying to his wealthy friends for aid. In judging this part of his conduct, one must bear in mind both his own doctrine about property, and the practice of the age. Godwin was a communist, and so, in some degree, were most of his friends. When he applied to Wedgwood, the philosophic potter of Etruria, or to Ritson, the vegetarian, or in later years to Shelley for money, he was simply giving virtue its occasion, and assisting property to find its level. He practised what he preached, and he would himself give with a generosity which seemed prodigal, to his own relatives, to promising young men, and even to total strangers. He supported one disciple at Cambridge, as he had educated

GODWIN AND SHELLEY 171

Cooper in his younger days. It was the prevailing theory of the age that men of genius have the right to call on society in the persons of its wealthier members for support. Helvétius, himself a rich man, had maintained this view. Southey and Coleridge acted on it. Dr. Priestley, universally respected both for his character and his talents, received large gifts from friends, admirers, members of his congregation and aristocratic patrons. To Godwin, profoundly individualistic as he was, a post in the civil service, or even a professorship, would have seemed a more degrading form of charity than this private benevolence.

Partly to mend his fortunes, partly to furnish himself with an occupation when his mind refused original work, Godwin in 1805 turned publisher. It was a disastrous inspiration, due apparently to his wife, who believed herself to possess a talent for business. The firm was established in Skinner Street, Holborn, and specialised in school books and children's tales. They were well-printed, and well-illustrated, and Godwin, writing under the pseudonym of Edward Baldwin, to avoid the odium which had now overtaken his own name, compiled a series of histories with his usual industry and conscientious finish.

Through years darkened with misfortune and clouded by failing health, he worked hard at the business of publishing. His capital was never adequate, though his friends and admirers twice came to his aid with public subscriptions. In 1822 he was evicted for arrears of rent, and in 1825 the unlucky venture came to an end.

These years were crowded with literary work, for neither " Baldwin " nor Godwin allowed their common pen to idle. Two elaborate historical works enjoyed and deserved a great reputation in their day, though subsequent research has rendered them obsolete—a *Life of Geoffrey Chaucer* (1803) and a *History of the Commonwealth of England from its Commencement to the Restoration of Charles II.* (1824-8). It is not easy for modern taste to do justice to Godwin's novels; but on them his contemporary fame chiefly rested, and publishers paid for them high though diminishing prices. They all belong to the romantic movement; some have a supernatural basis, and most of them discover a too obvious didactic purpose. *St. Leon* (1799), almost as popular in its day as *Caleb Williams*, mingles a romance of the elixir of life and the philosopher's stone with an ardent recommendation of those family affections which

GODWIN AND SHELLEY 173

Political Justice had depreciated. *Fleetwood* (1805) makes war on debauchery with sincere and impressive dulness. *Mandeville* (1817), *Cloudesley* (1830) and *Deloraine* (1833) are dead beyond the reach of curiosity, yet the Radical critics of his day, including Hazlitt, tried hard to convince themselves that Godwin was a greater novelist than the Tory, Scott. It remains to mention Godwin's two attempts to conquer the theatre with *Antonio* (1800) and *Faulkener* (1807). Neither play lived, and *Antonio*, written in a sort of journalese, cut up into blank verse lines, was too frigid to survive the first night. Godwin's disappointment would be comical if it were not painful. He regarded these deplorable tragedies as the flower of his genius.

Through these years of misfortune and eclipse, the friendships which Godwin could still retain were his chief consolation. The published letters of Coleridge and Lamb make a charming record of their intimacy. Whimsical and affectionate in their tone, they are an unconscious tribute as much to the man who received them as to the men who wrote them. Conservative critics have talked of Godwin's " coldness " because he could reason. But the abiding and generous regard of such a nature as Charles Lamb's is answer enough to these summary valuations. But Godwin's most characteristic relationship was with the young men who sought him out as an inspiration. He would write them long letters of advice, encouragement, and criticism, and despite his own poverty, would often relieve their distresses. The most interesting of them was an adventurous young Scot named Arnot who travelled on foot through the greater part of Europe during the Napoleonic wars. The tragedy which seemed always to pursue Godwin's intimates drove another of them, Patrickson, to suicide while an undergraduate at Cambridge. Bulwer Lytton, the last of these admiring young men, left a note on Godwin's conversational powers in his extreme old age, which assures us that he was "well worth hearing," even amid the brilliance of Lamb, Hunt, and Hazlitt, and could display "a grim jocularity of sarcasm."

One of these relationships has become historical, and has coloured the whole modern judgment of Godwin. It would be no exaggeration to say that Godwin formed Shelley's mind, and that *Prometheus Unbound* and *Hellas* were the greatest of Godwin's works. That debt is too often forgotten, while literary gossip loves to remind us that it was repaid in cheques and *post-obits*. The intellectual rela-

GODWIN AND SHELLEY 175

tionship will be discussed in a later chapter ; the bare facts of the personal connection must be told here. *Political Justice* took Shelley's mind captive while he was still at Eton, much as it had obsessed Coleridge, Southey, and Wordsworth. The influence with him was permanent ; and *Queen Mab* is nothing but Godwin in verse, with prose notes which quote or summarise him. A correspondence began in 1811, and the pupil met the master late in 1812, and again in 1813. They talked as usual of virtue and human perfectibility ; and as the intimacy grew, Shelley, whose chief employment at this time was to discover and relieve genius in distress, began to place his present resources and future prospects at Godwin's disposal. It was not an unnatural relationship to arise between a grateful disciple, heir to a great fortune, and a philosopher, aged, neglected, and sinking under the burden of debt.

Shelley's romantic runaway match with Harriet Westbrook had meanwhile entered on the period of misery and disillusion. She had lost her early love of books and ideas, had taken to hats and ostentation, and had become so harsh to him that he welcomed absence. It is certain that he believed her to be also in the vulgar sense of the word unfaithful. At this crisis, when the separation seemed already morally complete, he met Mary Godwin, who had been absent from home during most of his earlier visits. She was a young girl of seventeen, eager for knowledge and experience, and as her father described her, " singularly bold, somewhat imperious and active of mind," and " very pretty." They rapidly fell in love. Godwin's conduct was all that the most conventional morality could have required of him. His theoretical views of marriage were still unorthodox; he held at least that " the institution might with advantage admit of certain modifications." But nine years before in the preface to *Fleetwood* he had protested that he was " the last man to recommend a pitiful attempt by scattered examples to renovate the face of society." He seems, indeed, to have forgotten his own happy experiment with Mary Wollstonecraft, and protests with a vigour hardly to be expected from so stout an individualist against the idea, that " each man for himself should supersede and trample upon the institutions of the country in which he lives. A thousand things might be found excellent and salutary if brought into general practice, which would in some cases appear ridiculous and in others

GODWIN AND SHELLEY

attended with tragical consequences if prematurely acted upon by a solitary individual."

On this view he acted. He forbade Shelley his house, and tried to make a reconciliation between him and Harriet. On July 28, 1814, Mary secretly left her father's house, joined her lover, and began with him her life of ideal intimacy and devotion. Godwin felt and expressed the utmost disapproval, and for two years refused to meet Shelley, until at the close of 1816, after the suicide of the unhappy Harriet, he stood at his daughter's side as a witness to her marriage. His public conduct was correct. In private he continued to accept money from the erring disciple whom he refused to meet, and salved his elderly conscience by insisting that the cheques should be drawn in another name. There Godwin touched the lowest depths of his moral degeneration. Let us remember, however, that even Shelley, who saw the worst of Godwin, would never speak of him with total condemnation. "Added years," he wrote near the end of his life, "only add to my admiration of his intellectual powers, and even the moral resources of his character." In the poetical epistle to Maria Gisborne, he wrote of

> "That which was Godwin—greater none than he
> Though fallen, and fallen on evil times, to stand
> Among the spirits of our age and land
> Before the dread tribunal of To-come
> The foremost, while Rebuke cowers pale and dumb."

The end came to the old man amid comparative peace and serenity. He accepted a sinecure from the Whigs, and became a Yeoman Usher of the Exchequer, with a small stipend and chambers in New Palace Yard. It was a tribute as much to his harmlessness as to his merit. The work of his last years shows little decay in his intellectual powers. His *Thoughts on Man* (1831) collects his fugitive essays. They are varied in subject, suave, easy and conversational in manner, more polished in style than those of the *Enquirer*, if a good deal thinner in matter. They avoid political themes, but the ideal of human perfectibility none the less pervades the book with an unaggressive presence, a cold and wintry sun. One curious trait of his more cautious and conservative later mind is worth noting. When he wrote *Political Justice*, the horizons of science were unlimited, the vistas of discovery endless. Now he questions even the mathematical data of astronomy, talks of the limitations of our faculties, and applauds a positive attitude

GODWIN AND SHELLEY 179

that refrains from conjecture. His last years were spent in writing a book in which he ventured at length to state his views upon religion. Like Helvétius he perceived the advantages which an unpopular philosopher may derive from posthumous publication. Freed at last from the vulgar worries of debt and the tragical burden of personal ties, the fighting ended which had never brought him the joy of combat, the material struggle over which had issued in defeat, he became again the thing that was himself, a luminous intelligence, a humane thinker.

With eighty years of life behind him, and doubting whether the curtain of death concealed a secret, Godwin tranquilly faced extinction in April, 1836.

" To do my part to free the human mind from slavery," that in his own words was the main object of Godwin's life. The task was not fully discharged with the writing of *Political Justice*. He could never forget the terror and gloom of his own early years, and, like all the thinkers of the revolution, he coupled superstition with despotism and priests with kings as the arch-enemies of human liberty. The terrors of eternal punishment, the firmly riveted chains of Calvinistic logic, had fettered his own growing mind in youth ; and to the end he thought of traditional religion as the chief of those factitious things which prevent mankind from reaching the full stature to which nature destined it. Paine had attempted this work from a similar standpoint, but Godwin, with his trained speculative mind, and his ideal of courtesy and persuasiveness in argument, thought meanly (as a private letter shows) of his friend's polemics. It was an unlucky timidity which caused Mrs. Shelley to suppress her father's religious essays when the manuscript was bequeathed to her for publication on his death. When, at length, they appeared in 1873 (*Essays never before Published*), the work which they sought to accomplish had been done by other pens. They possess none the less an historical interest ; some fine pages will always be worth reading for their humane impulse and their manly eloquence ; they help us to understand the influence which Godwin's ideas, conveyed in personal intercourse, exerted on the author of *Prometheus Unbound*. There is little in them which a candid believer would resent to-day. Most of the dogmas which Godwin assailed have long

GODWIN AND SHELLEY

since crumbled away through the sapping of a humaner morality and a more historical interpretation of the Bible.

The book opens with a protest against the theory and practice of salutary delusions ; and Godwin once more pours his scorn upon those who would cherish their own private freedom, while preserving popular superstitions, " that the lower ranks may be kept in order." The foundation of all improvement is that " the whole community should run the generous race for intellectual and moral superiority." Godwin would preserve some portion of the religious sense, for we can reach sobriety and humility only by realising " how frail and insignificant a part we constitute of the great whole." But the fundamental tenets of dogmatic Christianity are far, he argues, from being salutary delusions. At the basis alike of Protestantism and Catholicism, he sees the doctrine of eternal punishment ; and with an iteration that was not superfluous in his own day, he denounces its cruel and demoralising effects. It saps the character where it is really believed, and renders the mind which receives it servile and pusillanimous. The case is no better when it is neither sincerely believed nor boldly rejected. Such an attitude, which is, he thinks, that of most professing believers, makes for insincerity, and for an indifference to all honest thought and speculation. The man who dare neither believe nor disbelieve is debarred from thinking at all.

Worst of all, this doctrine of endless torment and arbitrary election involves a blasphemous denial of the goodness of God. " To say all, then, in a word, since it must finally be told, the God of the Christians is a tyrant." He quotes the delightfully naïve reflection of Plutarch, who held that it was better to deny God than to calumniate Him, " for I had rather it should be said of me, that there was never such a man as Plutarch, than that it should be said that Plutarch was ill-natured, arbitrary, capricious, cruel, and inexorable." A survey of Church History brings out what Godwin calls " the mixed character of Christianity, its horrors and its graces." In much of what has come down to us from the Old Testament he sees the inevitable effects of anthropomorphism, when the religion of a barbarous age is reduced to writing, and handed down as the effect of inspiration. He cannot sufficiently admire the beauty of Christ's teaching of a perfect disinterestedness and self-denial—a doctrine in his own terminology of " universal benevolence." But the disciples lived in a preternatural atmosphere, continually busied with the four Last Things, death, judgment, heaven, and hell; and they distorted the beauty of the Christian morality by introducing an other-worldliness, to which the ancients had been strangers. From this came the despotism of the Church based on the everlasting burnings and the keys, and something of the spirit of St. Dominic and the Inquisition can be traced, he thinks, even to the earliest period of Christianity. The Gospel sermons do not always realise the Godwinian ideal of rational persuasion.

Godwin's own view is in the main what we should call agnostic: "I do not consider my faculties adequate to pronouncing upon the cause of all things. I am contented to take the phenomena as I behold them, without pretending to erect an hypothesis under the idea of making all things easy. I do not rest my globe of earth upon an elephant [a reference to the Indian myth], and the elephant upon a tortoise. I am content to take my globe of earth simply, in other words to observe the objects which present themselves to my senses, without undertaking to find out a cause why they are what they are."

With cautious steps, he will, however, go a

little further than this. He regards with reverence and awe " that principle, whatever it is, which acts everywhere around me." But he will not slide into anthropomorphism, nor give to this Supreme Thing, which recalls Shelley's Demogorgon, the shape of a man. " The principle is not intellect; its ways are not our ways." If there is no particular Providence, there is none the less a tendency in nature which seconds our strivings, guarantees the work of reason, and " in the vast sum of instances, works for good, and operates beneficially for us." The position reminds us of Matthew Arnold's definition of God as "the stream of tendency by which all things strive to fulfil the law of their being." "We have here," writes Godwin, "a secure alliance, a friend that so far as the system of things extends will never desert us, unhearing, inaccessible to importunity, uncapricious, without passions, without favour, affection, or partiality, that maketh its sun to rise on the evil and the good, and its rain to descend on the just and the unjust."

Amid the dim but rosy mist of this vague faith the old man went out to explore the unknown. A bolder and more rebellious thought was his real legacy to his age. It is the central impulse of the whole revolutionary school : " We know what we are : we know not what we might have been. But surely we should have been greater than we are but for this disadvantage [dogmatic religion, and particularly the doctrine of eternal punishment]. It is as if we took some minute poison with everything that was intended to nourish us. It is, we will suppose, of so mitigated a quality as never to have had the power to kill. But it may nevertheless stunt our growth, infuse a palsy into every one of our articulations, and insensibly change us from giants of mind which we might have been into a people of dwarfs."

Let us write Godwin's epitaph in his own Roman language. He stood erect and independent. He spoke what he deemed to be truth. He did his part to purge the veins of men of the subtle poisons which dwarf them.

CHAPTER VII

MARY WOLLSTONECRAFT

WHEN women, standing at length beyond the last of the gates and walls that have barred their road to freedom, measure their debt to history, there will be little to claim their gratitude before the close of the eighteenth century. The Protestant Reformation on the whole depressed their status, and even among its more speculative sects the Quakers stood alone in preaching the equality of the sexes. The English Whigs ignored the existence of women. It was left for the French thinkers who laid the foundations of the Revolution to formulate a view of society and human nature which, as it were, insisted on its own application to women. The idea of women's emancipation was alive among their principles. One can name its parents, and one marvels not at all that it seized this mind and the other, but that any mind among the professors of the " new philosophy " contrived to escape it. The central thought,

MARY WOLLSTONECRAFT 187

which inspired the gospel of perfectibility has a meaning for men which an enlightened mind can grasp, but it tells the plain obvious fact about women.

When Holcroft compares the influence of laws and institutions upon men to the action of beggars who mutilate their children, when Godwin talks of the subtle poisons of dogma and custom, which cause mankind to grow up a race of dwarfs when they should be giants, they seem to be using metaphors which describe nothing so well as the effect of an artificial education and a tradition of subjecttion upon women. One by one the thinkers of this generation were unconsciously laying down the premises which the women's movement needed. At the end of all their arguments for liberty and perfectibility, we seem to hear to-day a chorus of women's voices which points the application to themselves. There was little hope for women while the opinion prevailed that minds come into the world with their qualities innate and their limitations fixed by nature. If that were the case, then the undeniable fact that women were intellectually and morally dependent and inferior must be accepted as their inevitable destiny. Helvétius, all unconscious of what he did, was the hope-bringer, when he insisted that mind is the creation of education and experience. When he urged that the very inequality of men's talents is itself factitious and the result of more or less good fortune in the occasions which provoke a mind to activity, who could fail to enquire whether the accepted inferiority of women were so natural and so necessary as the whole world assumed ?

This school of thought revelled in social psychology. It studied in turn the soldier, the priest and the courtier, and shewed how each of these has a secondary character, a professional mind, a class morality impressed and imposed upon him by his education and employment. Looking down from the vantage ground of their philosophic salon upon their contemporaries in French society who owed their fortunes and reputations to the favour of an absolute court, Helvétius and his friends framed their general theory of the demoralisation which despotism brings about in the human character. They studied the natural history of the human parasite who flourished under the Bourbons. They need not have travelled to Versailles to find him. The domestic subjection of wives to husbands, the education of girls in a specialised morality, the fetters of custom and fashion, the experience of economic dependence, the denial of every noble stimulus to thought and action—these causes, more potent and more universal than any which work at Court, were making a sex condemned to an artificial inferiority, an induced parasitism. Thinkers who had discarded the notion that human minds come into the world with an innate character and with their limitations already predestined, were ripe to draw the conclusion. The Revolution believed that men by taking thought might add many cubits to their mental stature. To think in these terms was to prepare oneself to see that the " lovely follies " the " amiable weaknesses " of the " fair sex " were in their turn nothing innate, but the fostered characteristics of a class bred in subjection, the trading habits of a profession which had bent all its faculties to the art of pleasing. Reformers who sought to raise the peasant, the negro, and even the courtier to his full stature as a man, were inevitably led to consider the case of their own wives and daughters. They were not the men to be arrested by the distinction which has been recently invented. Democracy, we are told, is concerned with the removal not of natural, but of artificial inequalities. Their bias was to regard all inequalities as artificial. Looking forward to the goal of human perfection, they were prompt to realise that every advance would be insecure, and the final hope a delusion, if on their road they should leave half mankind behind them.

It requires a vigorous exercise of the historical imagination to realise the conditions which society imposed upon women in the eighteenth century. If Godwin and Paine had reflected closely on the position of women, they might have been led to modify their exaggerated antithesis between society and government. Government, indeed, imposed a barbarous code of laws upon women. It was a trifle that they were excluded from political power. The law treated a wife as the chattel of her husband, denied her the disposal of her own property, even when it was the produce of her own labour, sanctioned his use of violence to her person, and refused (as indeed it still in part does) to recognise her rights as a parent. But the state of the law reflected only too faithfully the opinions of society, and these opinions in their turn formed the minds of women. Civilised people amuse themselves to-day by detecting how much of the old prejudices still lurk in a shame-faced half-consciousness in the minds of modern men. There was no need in the eighteenth century for any fine analysis to detect the naïve belief that women exist only as auxiliary beings to contribute to the comfort and to flatter the self-esteem of men. The belief was avowed and accepted as the unquestioned basis of human society. Good men proclaimed it, and the cleverest women dared not question it.

For the crudest statement of it we need not go to men who defended despotism and convention in other departments of life. The most repulsive of all definitions of the principle of sex-subjection is to be found in Rousseau: —" The education of women should always be relative to that of men. To please, to be useful to us, to make us love and esteem them, to educate us when young, to take care of us when grown up, to advise, to console us, to render our lives easy and agreeable; these are the duties of women at all times, and what they should be taught in their infancy." When the men of the eighteenth century said this, they meant it, and they accepted not only its plain meaning, but its remotest logical consequences. It was a denial of the humanity and personality of women. A slave is a human being, whom the law deprives of his right to sell his labour. A woman had to learn that her subjection affected not only her relations to men, but her attitude to nature and to God. The subtle poison ran in her veins when she prayed and when she studied. Subject in her body, she was enslaved in mind and soul as well. Milton saw the husband as a priest intervening between a woman and her God :—

> He for God only, she for God in him.

Even on her knees a woman did not escape the consciousness of sex, and a manual of morality written by a learned divine (Dr. Fordyce) assured her that a "fine woman" never "strikes so deeply" as when a man sees her bent in prayer. She was encouraged to pray that she might be seen of men—men who scrutinised her with the eyes of desire. It is a woman, herself something of a "blue-stocking," who has left us the most pathetic statement of the intellectual fetters which her sex accepted. Women, says Mrs. Barbauld, "must often be content to know that a thing is so, without understanding the proof." They "cannot investigate; they may remember." She warns the girls whom she is addressing that if they will steal knowledge, they must learn, like the Spartan youths, to hide their furtive gains. "The thefts of knowledge in our sex are only connived at while carefully concealed, and if displayed punished with disgrace."

Religion was sullied; knowledge was closed; but above all the sentiment of the day perverted morals. Here, too, everything was relative to men, and men demanded a sensitive weakness, a shrinking timidity. Courage, honour, truth, sincerity, independence—these were items in a male ideal. They were to a woman as unnecessary, nay, as harmful in the marriage market as a sturdy frame and well-knit muscles. Dean Swift, a sharp satirist, but a good friend of women, comments on the prevailing view. "There is one infirmity," he writes in his illuminating *Letter to a very young lady on her marriage*, "which is generally allowed you, I mean that of cowardice," and he goes on to express what was in his day the wholly unorthodox view that "the same virtues equally become both sexes." There he was singular. The business of a woman was to cultivate those virtues most conducive to her prosperity in the one avocation open to her. That avocation was marriage, and the virtues were those which her prospective employer, the average over-sexed male, anxious at all points to feel his superiority, would desire in a subject wife. Submission was the first of them, and submission became the foundation of female virtue. Lord Kames, a forgotten but once popular

Scottish philosopher, put the point quite fairly (the quotation, together with that from Mrs. Barbauld, is to be found in Mr. Lyon Blease's valuable book on *The Emancipation of Englishwomen*): " Women, destined by nature to be obedient, ought to be disciplined early to bear wrongs without murmuring. . . . This is essential to the female sex, for ever subjected to the authority of a single person."

The rest of morality was summed up in the precepts of the art of pleasing. Chastity had, of course, its incidental place; it enhances the pride of possession. The art of pleasing was in practice a kind of furtive conquest by stratagems and wiles, by tears and blushes, in which the woman, by an assumed passivity, learned to excite the passions of the male. Rousseau owed much of his popularity to his artistic statement of this position:—" If woman be formed to please and to be subjected to man, it is her place, doubtless, to render herself agreeable to him. . . . The violence of his desires depends on her charms; it is by means of these that she should urge him to the exertion of those powers which nature hath given him. The most successful method of exciting them is to render such exertion necessary by resistance; as in that case self-love is added to desire, and the one triumphs in the victory which the other is obliged to acquire. Hence arise the various modes of attack and defence between 'the sexes; the boldness of one sex and the timidity of the other; and in a word, that bashfulness and modesty, with which nature hath armed the weak in order to subdue the strong."

The " soft," the " fair," the " gentle sex " learned its lesson with only too much docility. It grew up stunted to meet the prevailing demand. It acquired weakness, feigned ignorance, and emulated folly as sedulously as men will labour to make at least a show of strength, good sense, and knowledge. It adapted itself only too successfully to the economic conditions in which it found itself. Men accepted its flatteries and returned them with contempt. " Women," wrote that dictator of morals and manners, Lord Chesterfield, " are only children of a larger growth. . . . A man of sense only trifles with them, plays with them, humours and flatters them, as he does a sprightly, forward child." The men of that century valued women only as playthings. They forgot that he is the child who wants the toy.

The first protests against this morality

of degradation came, as one would expect, from men. Demoralising as it was for men, it did at least leave them the free use of their minds. Enquiry, reflection, scepticism, unsuitable if not immodest in a woman, were the rights of a manly intellect. Defoe and Swift uttered an unheeded protest in England, but neither of them carried the subject far. There are some good critical remarks in Helvétius about women's education; but the first man in that century who seemed to realise the importance and scope of what several dimly felt, was Baron Holbach, whose materialism was so peculiarly shocking to our forefathers. A chapter " On Women " in his *Système Social* (1774) opens thus: " In all the countries of the world the lot of women is to submit to tyranny. The savage makes a slave of his mate, and carries his contempt for her to the point of cruelty. For the jealous and voluptuous Asiatic, women are but the sensual instruments of his secret pleasures. . . . Does the European, in spite of the apparent deference which he affects towards women, really treat them with more respect? While we refuse them a sensible education, while we feed their minds with tedium and trifles, while we allow them to busy themselves only with playthings and fashions and adornments, while we seek to inspire them only with the taste for frivolous accomplishments, do we not show our real contempt, while we mask it with a show of deference and respect?"

Holbach was a rash and rather superficial metaphysician, but the warm-hearted and honest pages which follow this opening inspire a deep respect for the man. He talks of the absurdities of women's education; draws a bitter picture of a woman's fate in a loveless marriage of convenience; remarks that esteem is necessary for a happy marriage, but asks sadly how one is to esteem a mind which has emerged from a schooling in folly; assails the practice of gallantry, and the fashionable conjugal infidelities of his day; writes with real indignation of the dangers to which working-class girls are exposed; proposes to punish seduction as a crime no less cruel than murder, and concludes by confessing that he would like to adopt Plato's opinion that women should share with men in the tasks of government, but dreads the effects which would flow from the admission of the corrupt ladies of his day to power.

Twenty years later this promising beginning bore fruit in the mature and reasoned pleading of Condorcet for the reform of women's education. There was no subject on which this noble constructive mind insisted with such continual emphasis. His feminism (to use an ugly modern word), was an integral part of his thinking. He remembered women when he wrote of public affairs as naturally as most men forget them. He deserves in the gratitude of women a place at least as distinguished as John Stuart Mill's. The best and fullest statement of his position is to be found in the report and draft Bill on national education (Sur l'Instruction Publique), which he prepared for the Revolutionary Convention in 1792 (see also p. 109). He maintains boldly that the system of national education should be the same for women as for men. He specially insists that they should be admitted to the study of the natural sciences (these were days when it was held that a woman would lose her modesty if she studied botany), and thinks that they would render useful services to science, even if they did not attain the first rank. They ought to be educated for many reasons. They must be able to teach their children. If they remain ignorant, the curse of inequality will be introduced into the family, and mothers will be regarded by their sons with contempt. Nor will men retain their intellectual interests,

MARY WOLLSTONECRAFT

unless they can share them with women. Lastly, women have the same natural right to knowledge and enlightenment as men. The education should be given in common, and this will powerfully further the interests of morality. The separation of the sexes in youth really proceeds from the fear of unequal marriages, in other words, from avarice and pride. It would be dangerous for a democratic community to allow the spirit of social inequality to survive among women, with the consequence that it could never be extirpated among men. Condorcet was not a brilliant writer, but the humanity and generosity of his thought finds a powerful and reasoned expression in his sober and somewhat laboured sentences.

So far a good and enlightened man might go. The substance of all that need be said against the harem with the door ajar, in which the eighteenth century had confined the mind if not the body, of women, is to be found in Holbach and Condorcet. But they wrote from outside. They were the wise spectators who saw the consequences of the degradation of women, but did not intimately know its cause. Mary Wollstonecraft's *Vindication of the Rights of Woman* (1792) is perhaps the most original book of its century, not because its daring ideas were altogether new, but because in its pages for the first time a woman was attempting to use her own mind. Her ideas, as we have seen, were not absolutely new. They were latent in all the thinking of the revolutionary period. They had been foreshadowed by Holbach (whom she may have read), by Paine (whom she had occasionally met), and by Condorcet (whose chief contribution to the question, written in the same year as her *Vindication*, she obviously had not read). What was absolutely new in the world's history was that for the first time a woman dared to sit down to write a book which was not an echo of men's thinking, nor an attempt to do rather well what some man had done a little better, but a first exploration of the problems of society and morals from a standpoint which recognised humanity without ignoring sex. She showed her genius not so much in writing the book, which is, indeed, a faulty though an intensely vital performance, as in thinking out its position for herself.

She had her predecessors, but she owed to them little, if anything. There was not enough in them to have formed her mind, if she had come to their pages unemancipated. She freed herself from mental slavery, and the utmost which she can have derived from the two or three men who professed the same generous opinions, was the satisfaction of encouragement or confirmation. She owed to others only the powerful stimulus which the Revolution gave to all bold and progressive thought. The vitality of her ideas sprang from her own experience. She had received rather less than was customary of the slipshod superficial education permitted to girls of the middle classes in her day. With this nearly useless equipment, she had found herself compelled to struggle with the world not merely to gain a living, but to rescue a luckless family from a load of embarrassments and misfortunes. Her father was a drunkard, idle, improvident, moody and brutal, and as a girl she had often protected her mother from his violence. A sister had married a profligate husband, and Mary rescued her from a miserable home, in which she had been driven to temporary insanity. The sisters had attempted to live by conducting a suburban school for girls; a brief experience as a governess in a fashionable family had been even more formative.

When at length she took to writing and translating educational books, with the encouragement of a kindly publisher, she was practising under the stimulus of necessity the doctrine of economic independence, which became one of the foundations of her teaching. It is the pressure of economic necessity which in this generation and the last has forced women into a campaign for freedom and opportunity. What the growth of the industrial system has done for women in the mass, a hard experience did for Mary Wollstonecraft. In her own person or through her sisters she had felt in an aggravated form most of the wrongs to which women were peculiarly exposed. She had seen the reverse of the shield of chivalry, and known the domestic tyrannies of a sheltered home.

The miracle was that Mary Wollstonecraft's mind was never distorted by bitterness, nor her faith in mankind destroyed by cynicism. Her personality lives for us still in her own books and in the records of her friends. Opie's vivid painting hangs in the National Portrait Gallery to confirm what Godwin tells us of her beauty in his pathetic *Memoir* and to remind us of Southey's admiration for her eyes. Godwin writes of " that smile of bewitching tenderness . . . which won, both heart and soul, the affection of almost every one that beheld it." She was, he tells us, " in the best and most engaging sense, feminine in her manners"; and indeed her letters and her books present her to us as a woman who had courage and independence precisely because she was so normal, so healthy in mind and body, so richly endowed with a generous vitality. If she won the hearts of all who knew her, it was because her own affections were warm and true. She was a good sister, a good daughter, a passionate lover, an affectionate friend, a devoted and tender mother.

She was too real a human being to be misled by the impartialities of universal benevolence. " Few," she wrote, " have had much affection for mankind, who did not first love their parents, their brothers, sisters, and even the domestic brutes whom they first played with." That eloquent trait, her love of animals and her hatred of cruelty, helps to define her character. She was, says Godwin, " a worshipper of domestic life," and, for all her proud independence, in love with love. In Godwin's prim phraseology, she " set a great value on a mutual affection between persons of an opposite sex, and regarded it as the principal solace of human life." Indeed, in the *Letters to Imlay*, which appeared after her death, it is not so much the strength and independence of her final attitude which impresses us, as her readiness to forgive, her reluctance to resent his neglect, her affection which could survive so many proofs of the man's unworthiness. The strongest passion in her generous nature was maternal tenderness. It won her the enduring love of the children whom she taught as a governess. It caused her mind to be busied with the problem of education as its chief preoccupation. It informs her whole view of the rights and duties of women in her *Vindication*. It inspired the charming fragment entitled *Lessons for Little Fanny*, which is one of the most graceful expressions in English prose of the physical tenderness of a mother's love. If she despised the artificial sensibility which in her day was admired and cultivated by women, it was because her own emotions were natural and strong. Her intellect, which no regular discipline had formed, impressed the laborious and studious Godwin by its quickness and its flashes of sudden insight—its " intuitive perception of intellectual beauty."

The *Vindication* is certainly among the most remarkable books that have come down to us from that opulent age. It has in abundance most of the faults that a book can have. It was hastily written in six weeks.

It is ill-arranged, full of repetitions, full of digressions, and almost without a regular plan. Its style is unformed, sometimes rhetorical, sometimes familiar. But with all these faults, it teems with apt phrases, telling passages, vigorous sentences which sum up in a few convincing lines the substance of its message. It lacks the neatness, the athletic movement of Paine's English. It has nothing of the learning, the formidable argumentative compulsion of Godwin's writing. But it is sold to-day in cheap editions, while Godwin survives only on the dustier shelves of old libraries. Its passion and sincerity have kept it alive. It is the cry of an experience too real, too authentic, to allow of any meandering down the by-ways of fanciful speculation. It said with its solitary voice the thing which the main army of thinking women is saying to-day. There is scarcely a passage of its central doctrine which the modern leaders of the women's movement would repudiate or qualify; and there is little if anything which they would wish to add to it. Writers like Olive Schreiner, Miss Cicely Hamilton, and Mrs. Gilman have, indeed, a background of historical knowledge, an evolutionary view of society, a sense of the working of economic causes which Mary

Wollstonecraft did not possess and could not in her age have acquired, even if she had been what she was not, a woman of learning. But she has anticipated all their main positions, and formulated the ideal which the modern movement is struggling to complete. Her book is dated in every chapter. It is as much a page torn from the journals of the French Revolution as Paine's *Rights of Man* or Condorcet's *Sketch*. And yet it seems, as they do not, a modern book.

The chief merit of the *Vindication* is its clear perception that everything in the future of women depends on the revision of the attitude of men towards women and of women towards themselves. The rare men who saw this, from Holbach and Condorcet to Mill, were philosophers. Mary Wollstonecraft had no pretensions to philosophy. A brilliant courage gave her in its stead her range and breadth of vision. It would have been so much easier to write a treatise on education, a plea for the reform of marriage, or even an argument for the admission of women to political rights. To the last of these themes she alludes only in a single sentence: " I may excite laughter, by dropping a hint, which I mean to pursue, some future time, for I really think that women ought to have representatives, instead of being arbitrarily governed without having any direct share allowed them in the deliberations of government." She had the insight to perceive that the first task of the pioneer was to raise the whole broad issue of the subjection of her sex. She begins by linking her argument with a splendid imprudence to the revolutionary movement. It had proclaimed the supremacy of reason, and based freedom on natural right. Why was it that the new Constitution ignored women? With a fresh simplicity, she appeals to the French Convention in the name of its own abstract principles, as modern women appeal (with more experience of the limitations of male logic) to English Liberalism. But she knew very well what was the enormous despotism of interest and prejudice that she was attacking. The sensualist and the tyrant were for her interchangeable terms, and with great skill she enlists on her side the new passion for liberty. " All tyrants want to crush reason, from the weak king to the weak father." She demands the enlightenment of women, as the reformers demanded that of the masses. : " Strengthen the female mind by enlarging it, and there will be an end to blind obedience ; but as blind obedience is ever sought for by power, tyrants and sensualists are in the right when they endeavour to keep women in the dark, because the former only want slaves, and the latter a plaything."

With a shrewd if instinctive insight into social psychology, she traces to the unenlightened self-interest of the dominant sex the code of morals which has been imposed upon women. Rousseau supplies her with the perfect and finished statement of all that she opposed. He and his like had given a sex to virtue. She takes her stand on a broad human morality. " Freedom must strengthen the reason of woman until she comprehend her duty." Against the perverted sex-morality which treated woman in religion, in ethics, in manners as a being relative only to men, she directs the whole of her argument. It is "vain to expect virtue from women, till they are in some degree independent of men."

" Females have been insulated, as it were, and while they have been stripped of the virtue that should clothe humanity, they have been decked with artificial graces that enable them to exercise a short-lived tyranny. . . . Their sole ambition is to be fair, to raise emotion instead of inspiring respect;

MARY WOLLSTONECRAFT

and this ignoble desire, like the servility in absolute monarchies, destroys all strength of character. Liberty is the mother of virtue, and if women be, by their very constitution, slaves, and not allowed to breathe the sharp invigorating air of freedom, they must ever languish like exotics, and be reckoned beautiful flaws in nature. . . . Women, I allow, may have different duties to fulfil; but they are human duties. . . . If marriage be the cement of society, mankind should all be educated after the same model, or the intercourse of the sexes will never deserve the name of fellowship, nor will women ever fulfil the peculiar duties of their sex, till they become enlightened citizens, till they become free by being enabled to earn their own subsistence, independent of men; in the same manner, I mean, to prevent misconstruction, as one man is independent of another. Nay, marriage will never be held sacred till women, by being brought up with men, are prepared to be their companions rather than their mistresses."

It is a brave but singularly balanced view of human life and society. There is in it no trace of the dogmatic individualism that distorts the speculations of Godwin and clogs the more practical thinking of Paine. It is, indeed, a protest against the exaggeration of sex, which instilled in women "the desire of being always women." It flouts that external morality of reputation, which would have a woman always " seem to be this and that," because her whole status in the world depended on the opinion which men held of her. It demands in words which anticipate Ibsen's *Doll's House*, that a woman shall be herself and lead her own life. But " her own life " was for Mary Wollstonecraft a social life. The ideal is the perfect companionship of men and women, and the preparation of men and women, by an equal practice of modesty and chastity, and an equal advance in education, to be the parents of their children. She is ready indeed to rest her whole case for the education of women upon the duties of maternity. " Whatever tends to incapacitate the maternal character takes woman out of her sphere." The education which she demanded was the co-education of men and women in common schools. She attacked the dual standard of sexual morality with a brave plainness of speech. She demanded the opening of suitable trades and professions to women. She exposed the whole system which compels women to " live by their charm." But a less destructive reformer never set out to overthrow conventions. For her the duty always underlies the right, and the development of the self-reliant individual is a preparation for the life of fellowship.

CHAPTER VIII

SHELLEY

IF it were possible to blot out from our mind its memory of the Bible and of Protestant theology, and with that mind of artificial vacancy to read *Paradise Lost* and *Samson Agonistes*, how strange and great and mad would the genius of Milton appear. We should wonder at his creative mythological imagination, but we should marvel past all comprehending at his conceptions of the divine order, and the destiny of man. To attempt to understand Shelley without the aid of Godwin is a task hardly more promising than it would be to read Milton without the Bible.

The parallel is so close that one is tempted to pursue it further, for there is between these two poets a close sympathy amid glaring contrasts. Each admitted in spite of his passion for an ideal world an absorbing concern in human affairs, and a vehement interest in the contemporary struggle for liberty. If the one was a Republican Puritan and the other an anarchical atheist, the dress which their passion for liberty assumed was the uniform of the day. Neither was an original thinker. Each steeped himself in the classics. But more important even than the classics in the influences which moulded their minds, were the dogmatic systems to which they attached themselves. It is not the power of novel and pioneer thought which distinguishes a philosophical from a purely sensuous mind. Shelley no more innovated or created in metaphysics or politics than did Milton. But each had, with his gift of imagery, and his power of musical speech, an intellectual view of the universe. The name of Milton suggests to us eloquent rhythms and images which pose like Grecian sculpture. But Milton's world was the world as the grave, gowned men saw it who composed the Westminster Confession. The name of Shelley rings like the dying fall of a song, or floats before our eyes amid the faery shapes of wind-tossed clouds. But Shelley's world was the world of the utilitarian Godwin and the mathematical Condorcet. The supremacy of an intellectual vision is not a common characteristic among poets, but it raises Milton and Shelley to the choir in which Dante and Goethe are leaders.

For Keats beauty was truth, and that was all he cared to know. Coleridge, indeed, was a metaphysician of some pretensions, but the " honey dew " on which he fed when he wrote *Christabel* and *Kubla Khan* was not the *Critique of Pure Reason*. But to Shelley *Political Justice* was the veritable " milk of paradise." We must drink of it ourselves if we would share his banquet. Godwin in short explains Shelley, and it is equally true that Shelley is the indispensable commentary to Godwin. For all that was living and human in the philosopher he finds imaginative expression. His mind was a selective soil, in which only good seed could germinate. The flowers wear the colour of life and emotion. In the clear light of his verse, gleaming in their passionate hues, they display for us their values. Some of them, the bees of a working hive will consent to fertilise; from others they will turn decidedly away. Shelley is Godwin's fertile garden. From another standpoint he is the desert which Godwin laid waste.

It is, indeed, the commonplace of criticism to insist on the reality which the ideal world possessed for Shelley. Other poets have illustrated thought by sensuous imagery. To Shelley, thought alone was the essential thing. A good impulse, a dream, an idea, were for him what a Centaur or a Pegasus were for common fancy. He sees in *Prometheus Unbound* a spirit who

> Speeded hither on the sigh
> Of one who gave an enemy
> His plank, then plunged aside to die.

Another spirit rides on a sage's " dream with plumes of flame " ; and a third tells how a poet

> Will watch from dawn to gloom
> The lake-reflected sun illume,
> The yellow bees in the ivy-bloom,
> Nor heed, nor see, what things they be;
> But from these create he can
> Forms more real than living man,
> Nurslings of immortality.

How naturally from Shelley's imagination flowed the lines about Keats :—

> All he had loved and moulded into thought
> From shape and hue and odour and sweet sound
> Lamented Adonais.

This was no rhetoric, no affectation of fancy. Shelley saw the immortal shapes of " Desires and Adorations " lamenting over the bier of the mortal Keats, because for him an idea or a passion was incomparably more real and more comprehensible than the things of flesh and earth, of whose existence the senses persuade us. To such a mind philosophy was not a distant world to be entered with diffident and halting feet, ever ready to retreat at the first alarm of common-sense. It was his daily habitation. He lived in it, and guided himself by its intellectual compass among the perils and wonders of life, as naturally as other men feel their way by touch. This ardent, sensitive, emotional nature, with all its gift of lyrical speech and passionate feeling, was in fact the ideal man of the Godwinian conception, who lives by reason and obeys principles. Three men in modern times have achieved a certain fame by their rigid obedience to " rational " conceptions of conduct—Thomas Day, who wrote *Sandford and Merton*, Bentham, and Herbert Spencer. But the erratic, fanciful Shelley was as much the enthusiastic slave of reason, as any of these three; and he seemed erratic only because to be perfectly rational is in this world the wildest form of eccentricity. He came upon *Political Justice* while he was still a school-boy at Eton; and his diaries show that there hardly passed a year of his life in which he omitted to re-read it. Its phraseology colours his prose; his mind was built upon it, as Milton's was upon the Bible. We hardly require his own confession to

SHELLEY

assure us of the debt. " The name of Godwin," he wrote in 1812, " has been used to excite in me feelings of reverence and admiration. I have been accustomed to consider him a luminary too dazzling for the darkness which surrounds him. From the earliest period of my knowledge of his principles, I have ardently desired to share on the footing of intimacy that intellect which I have delighted to contemplate in its emanations. Considering then, these feelings, you will not be surprised at the inconceivable emotions with which I learnt your existence and your dwelling. I had enrolled your name in the list of the honourable dead. I had felt regret that the glory of your being had passed from this earth of ours. It is not so. You still live, and I firmly believe are still planning the welfare of human kind."

The enthusiastic youth was to learn that his master's preoccupation was with concerns more sordid and more pressing than the welfare of human kind ; but if close personal intercourse brought some disillusionment regarding Godwin's private character, it only deepened his intellectual influence, and confirmed Shelley's lifelong adhesion to his system. No contemporary thinker ever contested Godwin's empire over Shelley's mind; and if in later years Plato claimed an ever-growing share in his thoughts, we must remember that in several of his fundamental tenets Godwin was a Platonist without knowing it. It is only in his purely personal utterances, in the lyrics which rendered a mood or an impression, or in such fancies as the *Witch of Atlas*, that Shelley can escape from the obsession of *Political Justice*. The voice of Godwin does not disturb us in *The Skylark*, and it is silenced by the violent passions of *The Cenci*. But in all the more formal and graver utterances of Shelley's genius, from *Queen Mab* to *Hellas*, it supplies the theme and Shelley writes the variations. *Queen Mab*, indeed, is nothing but a fervent lad's attempt to state in verse the burden of Godwin's prose. Some passages in it (notably the lines about commerce) are a mere paraphrase or summary of pages from *The Enquirer* or *Political Justice*. In the *Revolt of Islam*, and still more in *Prometheus Unbound*, Shelley's imagination is becoming its own master. The variations are more important, more subtle, more beautiful than the theme; but still the theme is there, a precise and definite dogma for fancy to embroider. It is only in *Hellas* that Shelley's power of narrative (in Hassan's story), his irrepressible lyrical gift, and his passion which at length could speak in its own idiom, combine to make a masterpiece which owes to Godwin only some general ideas. If the transcript became less literal, it was not that the influence had waned. It was rather that Shelley was gaining the full mastery of his own native powers of expression. In these poems he assumes or preaches all Godwin's characteristic doctrines, perfectibility, non-resistance, anarchism, communism, the power of reason and the superiority of persuasion over force, universal benevolence, and the ascription of moral evil to the desolating influence of " positive institution."

The general agreement is so obvious that one need hardly illustrate it. What is more curious is the habit which Shelley acquired of reproducing even the minor opinions or illustrations which had struck him in his continual reading of Godwin. When Mammon advises Swellfoot the Tyrant to refresh himself with

> A simple kickshaw by your Persian cook
> Such as is served at the Great King's second table,
> The price and pains which its ingredients cost
> Might have maintained some dozen families
> A winter or two—not more.

he is simply making an ironical paraphrase from Godwin. The fine scene in Canto XI.

of the *Revolt of Islam*, in which Laon, confronting the tyrant on his throne, quells by a look and a word a henchman who was about to stab him, is a too brief rendering of Godwin's reflections on the story of Marius and the Executioner (see p. 128).

> And one more daring, raised his steel anew
> To pierce the stranger: "What hast thou to do
> With me, poor wretch?"—calm, solemn and severe
> That voice unstrung his sinews, and he threw
> His dagger on the ground, and pale with fear,
> Sate silently.

The pages of Shelley are littered with such reminiscences.

Matthew Arnold said of Shelley that he was "a beautiful and ineffectual angel beating in the void his luminous wings in vain." One is tempted to retort that to be beautiful is in itself to escape futility, and to people a void with angels is to be far from ineffectual. But the metaphor is more striking as phrase-making than as criticism. The world into which the angel fell, wide-eyed, indignant, and surprised, was not a void. It was a nightmare composed of all the things which to common mortals are usual, normal, inevitable—oppressions and wars, follies and crimes, kings and priests, hangmen and inquisitors, poverty and luxury. If he beat his wings in this cage of horrors, it was with the rage and terror of a bird which belongs to the free air. Shelley, Matthew Arnold held, was not quite sane. Sanity is a capacity for becoming accustomed to the monstrous. Not time nor grey hairs could bring that kind of sanity to Shelley's clear-sighted madness. If he must be compared to an angel, Mr. Wells has drawn him for us. He was the angel whom a country clergyman shot in mistake for a buzzard, in that graceful satire, *The Wonderful Visit*. Brought to earth by this mischance, he saw our follies and our crimes without the dulling influence of custom. Satirists have loved to imagine such a being. Voltaire drew him with as much wit as insight in *L'Ingénu*—the American savage who landed in France, and made the amazing discovery of civilisation. Shelley had not dropped from the clouds nor voyaged from the backwoods, but he seems always to be discovering civilisation with a fresh wonder and an insatiable indignation.

One may doubt whether a saint has ever lived more selfless, more devoted to the beauty of virtue; but one quality Shelley lacked which is commonly counted a virtue. He had none of that imaginative sympathy which can make its own the motives and desires of other men. Self-interest, intolerance and greed he understood as little as common men understand heroism and devotion. He had no mean powers of observation. He saw the world as it was, and perhaps he rather exaggerated than minimised its ugliness. But it never struck him that its follies and crimes were human failings and the outcome of anything that is natural in the species. The doctrines of perfectibility and universal benevolence clothed themselves for him in the Godwinian phraseology, but they were the instinctive beliefs of his temperament. So sure was he of his own goodness, so natural was it with him to love and to be brave, that he unhesitatingly ascribed all the evil of the world to the working of some force which was unnatural, accidental, anti-human. If he had grown up a mediæval Christian, he would have found no difficulty in blaming the Devil. The belief was in his heart; the formula was Godwin's. For the wonder, the miracle of all this unnatural, incomprehensible evil in the world, he found a complete explanation in the doctrine that "positive institutions" have poisoned and distorted the natural good in man. After a gloomy picture in *Queen Mab* of all the oppressions which are done under the sun, he suddenly breaks away to absolve nature:

> Nature !—No !
> Kings, priests and statesmen blast the human flower
> Even in its tender bud; their influence darts
> Like subtle poison through the bloodless veins
> Of desolate society. . . .
> Let priest-led slaves cease to proclaim that man
> Inherits vice and misery, when force
> And falsehood hang even o'er the cradled babe
> Stifling with rudest grasp all natural good.

It is a stimulating doctrine, for if humanity had only to rid itself of kings and priests, the journey to perfection would be at once brief and eventful. As a sociological theory it is unluckily unsatisfying. There is, after all, nothing more natural than a king. He is a zoological fact, with his parallel in every herd of prairie dogs. Nor is there anything much more human than the tendency to convention which gives to institutions their rigidity. If force and imposture have had a share in the making of kings and priests, it is equally true that they are the creation of the servility and superstition of the mass of men. The eighteenth century chose to forget that man is a gregarious animal. Oppression and priestcraft are the transitory forms in which the flock has sought to cement its union. But the modern world is steeped in the lore of anthropology; there is little need to bring its heavy guns to bear upon the slender fabric of Shelley's dream. *Queen Mab* was a boy's precocious effort, and in later verses Shelley put the case for his view of evil in a more persuasive form. He is now less concerned to declare that it is unnatural, than to insist that it flows from defects in men which are not inherent or irremovable. The view is stated with pessimistic malice by a Fury in *Prometheus Unbound* after a vision of slaughter.

FURY.

Blood thou can'st see, and fire; and can'st hear groans.
Worse things unheard, unseen, remain behind.

PROMETHEUS.

Worse ?

FURY.

In each human heart terror survives
The ravin it has gorged: the loftiest fear,
All that they would disdain to think were true :
Hypocrisy and custom make their minds
The fanes of many a worship, now outworn.
They dare not devise good for man's estate,
And yet they know not that they do not dare.
The good want power, but to weep barren tears.
The powerful goodness want—worse need for them.
The wise want love; and those who love want wisdom,
And all best things are thus confused to ill.
Many are strong and rich, and would be just,
But live among their suffering fellow-men
As if none felt; they know not what they do.

Shelley so separated the good and evil in the world, that he was presently vexed as acutely as any theist with the problem of accounting for evil. Paine felt no difficulty in his sharp, positive mind. He traced all the wrongs of society to the egoism of priests and kings; and, since he did not assume the fundamental goodness of human nature, it troubled none of his theories to accept the crude primitive fact of self-interest. What Shelley would really have said in answer to a question about the origin of evil, if we had found him in a prosaic mood, it is hard to guess, and the speculation does not interest us. Shelley's prose opinions were of no importance. What we do trace in his poetry is a tendency, half conscious, uttering itself only in figures and parables, to read the riddle of the universe as a struggle between two hostile principles. In the world of prose he called himself an atheist. He rejoiced in the name, and used it primarily as a challenge to intolerance. " It is a good word of abuse to stop discussion," he said once to his friend Trelawny, " a painted devil to frighten the foolish, a threat to intimidate the wise and good. I used it to express my abhorrence of superstition. I took up the word as a knight takes up a gauntlet in defiance of injustice."

Shelley was an atheist because Christians used the name of God to sanctify persecution. That was really his ultimate emotional reason. His mythology, when he came to paint the world in myths, was Manichean. His creed was an ardent dualism, in which a God and an anti-God contend and make history. But in his mood of revolt it suited him to confuse the names and the symbols. The snake is everywhere in his poems the incarnation of good, and if we ask why, there is probably no other reason than that the Hebrew mythology against which he revolted, had taken it as the symbol of evil. The legitimate Gods in his Pantheon are always in the wrong. He belongs to the cosmic party of opposition, and the Jupiter of his *Prometheus* is morally a temporarily omnipotent devil. Like Godwin he felt that the God of orthodoxy was a " tyrant," and he revolted against Him, because he condemned the world which He had made.

The whole point of view, as it concerns Christian theology, is stated with a bitter clearness, in the speech of Ahasuerus in *Queen Mab*. The first Canto of the *Revolt of Islam* puts the position of dualism without reserve :

Know, then, that from the depths of ages old
Two Powers o'er mortal things dominion hold,
Ruling the world with a divided lot,
Immortal, all-pervading, manifold,
Twin Genii, equal Gods—when life and thought
Sprang forth, they burst the womb of inessential Nought.

The good principle was the Morning Star (as though to remind us of Lucifer) until his enemy changed him to the form of a snake. The anti-God, whom men worship blindly as God, holds sway over our world. Terror, madness, crime, and pain are his creation, and Asia in *Prometheus* cries aloud—

Utter his name: a world pining in pain
Asks but his name: curses shall drag him down.

In the sublime mythology of *Prometheus* the war of God and anti-God is seen visibly, making the horrors of history. As Jupiter's Furies rend the heart of the merciful Titan chained to his rock on Caucasus, murders and crucifixions are enacted in the world below. The mythical cruelties in the clouds are the shadows of man's sufferings below; and they are also the cause. A mystical parallelism links the drama in Heaven with the tragedy on earth; we suffer from the malignity of the World's Ruler, and triumph by the endurance of Man's Saviour.

Nothing could be more absurd than to call Shelley a Pantheist. Pantheism is the creed of conservatism and resignation. Shelley felt the world as struggle and revolt, and like all the poets, he used Heaven as the vast canvas on which to paint with a demonic brush an heroic idealisation of what he saw below. It would be interesting to know whether any human heart, however stout and rebellious, when once it saw the cosmic process as struggle, has ever been able to think of the issue as uncertain. Certainly for Shelley there was never a doubt about the final triumph of good. Godwin qualified his agnosticism by supposing that there was a tendency in things (he would not call it spiritual, or endow it with mind) which somehow co-operates with us and assures the victory of life (see p. 184). One seems to meet this vague principle, this reverend Thing, in Shelley's Demogorgon, the shapeless, awful negation which overthrows the maleficent Jupiter, and with his fall inaugurates the golden age. The strange name of Demogorgon has probably its origin in the clerical error of some mediæval copyist, fumbling with the scholia of an anonymous grammarian. One can conceive that it appealed to Shelley's wayward fancy because it suggested none of the traditional theologies; and certainly it has a mysterious and venerable sound. Shelley can describe It only as Godwin describes his principle by a series of negatives.

> I see a mighty darkness
> Filling the seat of power, and rays of gloom
> Dart round, as light from the meridian sun,
> Ungazed upon and shapeless; neither limb,
> Nor form, nor outline; yet we feel it is
> A living spirit.

It is the eternal X which the human spirit always assumes when it is at a loss to balance its equations. Demogorgon is, because if It were not, our strivings would be a battle in the mist, with no clear trumpet-note that promised triumph. Shelley, turning amid his singing to the supremest of all creative work, the making of a mythology, invents his God very much as those detested impostors, the primitive priests, had done. He gives Humanity a friendly Power as they had endowed their tribe with a god of battles. Humanity at grips with chaos is curiously like a nigger clan in the bush. It needs a fetish of victory. But a poet's mythology is to be judged by its fruits. A faith is worth the cathedral it builds. A myth is worth the poem it inspires.

If Shelley's ultimate view of reality is

vague, a thing to be shadowed in myths and hinted in symbols, there is nothing indefinite in his view of the destinies of mankind. Here he marched behind Godwin, and Godwin hated vagueness. His intellect had assimilated all the steps in the argument for perfectibility. It emerges in places in its most dogmatic form. Institutions make us what we are, and to free us from their shackles is to liberate virtue and unleash genius. He pauses midway in the preface to *Prometheus* to assure us that, if England were divided into forty republics, each would produce philosophers and poets as great and numerous as those of Athens. The road to perfection, however, is not through revolution, but by the gradual extirpation of error. When he writes in prose, he expresses himself with all the rather affected intellectualism of the Godwinian psychology. " Revenge and retaliation," he remarks in the preface to *The Cenci*, " are pernicious *mistakes*." But temperament counts for something even in a disciple so devout as Shelley. He had an intellectual view of the world ; but, when once the rhythm of his musical verse had excited his mind to be itself, the force and simplicity of his emotion transfuse and transform these abstractions. Godwin's "universal benevolence" was with him an ardent affectionate love for his kind. Godwin's cold precept that it was the duty of an illuminated understanding to contribute towards the progress of enquiry, by arguing about perfection and the powers of the mind in select circles of friends who meet for debate, but never (virtue forbids) for action, became for him a zealous missionary call.

One smiles, with his irreverent yet admiring biographers, at the early escapades of the married boy—the visit to Dublin at the height of the agitation for Catholic emancipation, the printing of his Address to the Irish Nation, and his trick of scattering it by flinging copies from his balcony at passersby, his quaint attempts to persuade grave Catholic noblemen that what they ought really to desire was a total and rapid transformation of the whole fabric of society, his efforts to found an association for the moral regeneration of mankind, and his elfish amusement of launching the truth upon the waters in the form of pamphlets sealed up in bottles. Shelley at this age perpetrated "rags" upon the universe, much as commonplace youths make hay of their fellows' rooms. It is amusing to read the solemn letters in which Godwin, complacently accepting the post of mentor, tells Shelley that he is much too young to reform the world, urges him to acquire a vicarious maturity by reading history, and refers him to *Political Justice passim* for the arguments which demonstrate the error of any attempt to improve mankind by forming political associations.

It is questionable how far the world has to thank Godwin for dissuading ardent young men from any practical effort to realise their ideals. It is just conceivable that, if the generation which hailed him as prophet had been stimulated by him to do something more than fold its hands in an almost superstitious veneration for the Slow Approach of Truth, there might have arisen under educated leaders some movement less class-bound than Whig Reform, less limited than the Corn Law agitation, and more intelligent than Chartism. But, if politics lost by Godwin's quietism, literature gained. It was Godwin's mission in life to save poets from Botany Bay; he rescued Shelley, as he had rescued Southey and Coleridge. It was by scattering his pity and his sympathy on every living creature around him, and squandering his fortune and his expectations in charity, while he dodged the duns and lived on bread and tea, that Shelley followed in action the

SHELLEY

principles of universal benevolence. Godwin omitted the beasts; but Shelley, practising vegetarianism and buying crayfish in order to return them to the river, realised the " boast " of the poet in *Alastor*:—

> If no bright bird, insect, or gentle beast
> I consciously have injured, but still loved
> And cherished these my kindred—

We hear of his gifts of blankets to the poor lace-makers at Marlow, and meet him stumbling home barefoot in mid-winter because he had given his boots to a poor woman.

Perhaps the most characteristic picture of this aspect of Shelley is Leigh Hunt's anecdote of a scene on Hampstead Heath. Finding a poor woman in a fit on the top of the Heath, Shelley carries her in his arms to the lighted door of the nearest house, and begs for shelter. The householder slams it in his face, with an " impostors swarm everywhere," and a " Sir, your conduct is extraordinary."

" Sir," cried Shelley, " I am sorry to say that *your* conduct is not extraordinary. . . It is such men as you who madden the spirits and the patience of the poor and wretched; and if ever a convulsion comes in this country (which is very probable), recollect what I tell you. You will have your house, that you refuse to put this miserable woman into, burnt over your head."

It must have been about this very time that the law of England (quite content to regard the owner of the closed door as a virtuous citizen) decided that the Shelley who carried this poor stranger into shelter, fetched a doctor, and out of his own poverty relieved her direr need, was unfit to bring up his own children.

If Shelley allowed himself to be persuaded by Godwin to abandon his missionary adventures, he pursued the ideal in his poems. Whether by Platonic influence, or by the instinct of his own temperament, he moves half-consciously from the Godwinian notion that mankind are to be reasoned into perfection. The contemplation of beauty is with him the first stage in the progress towards reasoned virtue. " My purpose," he writes in the preface to *Prometheus*, " has been . . . to familiarise . . . poetical readers with beautiful idealisms of moral excellence; aware that, until the mind can love, and admire, and trust, and hope, and endure, reasoned principles of moral conduct are seeds cast upon the highway of life, which the unconscious passenger tramples into dust, although they would bear the harvest of his happiness." It was for want of virtue, as Mary Wollstonecraft reflected, writing sadly after the Terror, that the French Revolution had failed. The lesson of all the horrors of oppression and reaction which Shelley described, the comfort of all the listening spirits who watch from their mental eyries the slow progress of mankind to perfection, the example of martyred patriots—these tend always to the moral which Demogorgon sums up at the end of the unflagging, unearthly beauties of the last triumphant act of *Prometheus Unbound*:

> To suffer woes which Hope thinks infinite;
> To forgive wrongs darker than death or night;
> To defy Power, which seems omnipotent;
> To love and bear; to hope till Hope creates
> From its own wreck the thing it contemplates;
> Neither to change, nor falter, nor repent;
> This like thy glory, Titan! is to be
> Good, great and joyous, beautiful and free;
> This is alone Life, Joy, Empire, and Victory.

To suffer, to forgive, to love, but above all, to defy—that was for Shelley the whole duty of man.

In two peculiarities, which he constantly emphasised, Shelley's view of progress differed at once from Godwin's conception, and from the notion of a slow evolutionary growth which the men of to-day consider historical he traced the impulse which is to lead mankind to perfection, to the magnetic leading of chosen and consecrated spirits. He saw the process of change not as a slow evolution (as moderns do), nor yet as the deliberate discarding of error at the bidding of rational argument (as Godwin did), but rather as a sudden emotional conversion. The missionary is always the light-bringer. "Some eminent in virtue shall start up," he prophesies in *Queen Mab*. The *Revolt of Islam*, so puzzling to the uninitiated reader by the wilful inversions of its mythology, and its history which seems to belong to no conceivable race of men, becomes, when one grasps its underlying ideas, a luminous epic of revolutionary faith, precious if only because it is told in that elaborately musical Spenserian stanza which no poet before or after Shelley has handled with such easy mastery. Their mission to free their countrymen comes to Laon and Cythna while they are still children, brooding over the slavery of modern Greece amid the ruins of a free past. They dream neither of teaching nor of fighting. They are the winged children of Justice and Truth, whose mere words can scatter the thrones of the oppressor, and trample the last altar

SHELLEY

in the dust. It is enough to speak the name of Liberty in a ship at sea, and all the coasts around it will thrill with the rumour of her name. In one moving, eloquent harangue, Cythna converts the sailors of the ship, laden with slaves and the gains of commerce, into the pioneers of her army. She paints to them the misery of their own lot, and then appeals to the central article of revolutionary faith:

> This need not be; ye might arise and will
> That gold should lose its power and thrones their glory,
> That love which none may bind be free to fill
> The world like light; and evil faith, grown hoary
> With crime, be quenched and die.

"Ye might arise and will"—it was the inevitable corollary of the facile analysis which traced all the woes of mankind not to "nature," but to kings, priests, and institutions. Shelley's missionaries of liberty preach to a nation of slaves, as the apostles of the Salvation Army preach in the slums to creatures reared in degradation, the same mesmeric appeal. Conversion is a psychological possibility, and the history of revolutions teaches its limitations and its power as instructively as the history of religion. It breaks down not because men are incapable of the sudden effort that can "arise and will," but rather because to render its effects permanent, it must proceed to regiment the converts in organised associations, which speedily develop all the evils that have ruined the despotism it set out to overthrow.

The interest of this revolutionary epic lies largely in the marriage of Godwin's ideas with Mary Wollstonecraft's, which in the second generation bears its full imaginative fruit. The most eloquent verses are those which describe Cythna's leadership of the women in the national revolt, and enforce the theme " Can man be free, if woman be a slave ? " Not less characteristic is the Godwinian abhorrence of violence, and the Godwinian trust in the magic of courageous passivity. Laon finds the revolutionary hosts about to slaughter their vanquished oppressors, and persuades them to mercy and fraternity with the appeal.

> O wherefore should ill ever flow from ill
> And pain still keener pain for ever breed.

He pardons and spares the tyrant himself; and Cythna shames the slaves who are sent to bind her, until they weep in a sudden perception of the beauty of virtue and courage. When the reaction breaks at length upon the victorious liberators, they stand passive to be hewn down, as Shelley, in the *Masque of*

Anarchy, written after Peterloo, advised the English reformers to do.

> With folded arms and steady eyes,
> And little fear and less surprise,
> Look upon them as they slay,
> Till their rage has died away.
>
> Then they will return with shame
> To the place from which they came,
> And the blood thus shed will speak
> In hot blushes on their cheek.

The simple stanzas might have been written by Blake. There is something in the primitive Christianity of this aggressive Atheist which breathes the childlike innocence of the Kingdom of Heaven. Shelley dreamed of "a nation made free by love." With a strange mystical insight, he stepped beyond the range of the Godwinian ethics, when he conceived of his humane missionaries as victims who offer themselves a living sacrifice for the redemption of mankind. Prometheus chained to his rock, because he loved and defied, by some inscrutable magic of destiny, brings at last by his calm endurance the consummation of the Golden Age. Laon walks voluntarily on to the pile which the Spanish inquisitor had heaped for him; and Cythna flings herself upon the flames in a last affirmation of the power of self-sacrifice and the beauty of comradeship.

Thrice Shelley essayed to paint the state of perfection which mankind might attain, when once it should " arise and will." The first of the three pictures is the most literally Godwinian. It is the boyish sketch of *Queen Mab*, with pantisocracy faithfully touched in, and Godwin's speculations on the improvement of the human frame suggested in a few pregnant lines. One does not feel that Shelley's mind is even yet its own master in the firmer and maturer picture which concludes the third act of *Prometheus Unbound*. He is still repeating a lesson, and it calls forth less than the full powers of his imagination. The picture of perfection itself is cold, negative, and mediocre. The real genius of the poet breaks forth only when he allows himself in the fourth act to sing the rapture of the happy spirits who " bear Time to his tomb in eternity," while they circle in lyrical joy around the liberated earth. There sings Shelley. The picture itself is a faithful illustration etched with a skilful needle to adorn the last chapter of *Political Justice*. Evil is once more and always something factitious and unessential. The Spirit of the Earth sees the " ugly human shapes and visages" which men had worn in the old bad days float away through the air like chaff on the wind. They were no more than masks. Thrones are kingless, and forthwith men walk in upright equality, neither fawning nor trembling. Republican sincerity informs their speech:

> None talked that common false cold hollow talk
> Which makes the heart deny the yes it breathes.

Women are "changed to all they dared not be," and "speak the wisdom once they could not think." "Thrones, altars, judgment-seats and prisons," and all the "tomes of reasoned wrong, glozed on by ignorance" cumber the ground like the unnoticed ruins of a barbaric past.

> The loathsome mask has fallen, the man remains
> Sceptreless, free, uncircumscribed, but man
> Equal, unclassed, tribeless and nationless
> Exempt from awe, worship, degree, the king
> Over himself; just, gentle, wise: but man
> Passionless.

The story ends there, and if we do not so much as wait for the assurance that man passionless, tribeless, and nationless lived happily ever afterwards, it is because we are unable to feel even this faint interest in his destiny. There is something amiss with an ideal which is constrained to express itself in negatives. What should be the climax of a triumphant argument becomes its refutation. To reduce ourselves to this abstract quintessential man might be euthanasia. It would not be paradise.

The third of Shelley's visions of perfection is the climax of *Hellas*. One feels in attempting to make about *Hellas* any statement in bald prose, the same sense of baffled incompetence that a modest mind experiences in attempting to describe music. One reads what the critics have written about Beethoven's Heroic Symphony, to close the page wondering that men with ears should have dared to write it. The insistent rhythm beats in your blood, the absorbing melodies obsess your brain, and you turn away realising that emotion, when it can find a channel of sense, has a power which defies the analytic understanding. *Hellas*, in a sense, is absolute poetry, as the " Eroica " is absolute music. Ponder a few lines in one of the choruses which seem to convey a definite idea, and against your will the elaborate rhythms and rhymes will carry you along, until thought ceases and only the music and the picture hold your imagination.

And yet Shelley meant something as certainly as Beethoven did. Nowhere is his genius so realistic, so closely in touch with contemporary fact, yet nowhere does he soar so easily into his own ideal world. He conceived it while Mavrocordato, about to start to fight for the liberation of Greece, was paying daily visits to Shelley's circle at Pisa. The events in Turkey, now awful, now hopeful, were before him as crude facts in the newspaper. The historians of classical Greece were his continual study. As he steeped himself in Plato, a world of ideal forms opened before him in a timeless heaven as real as history, as actual as the newspapers. *Hellas* is the vision of a mind which touches fact through sense, but makes of sense the gate and avenue into an immortal world of thought. Past and present and future are fused in one glowing symphony. The Sultan is no more real than Xerxes, and the golden consummation glitters with a splendour as dazzling and as present as the Age of Pericles. For Shelley, this denial of time had become a conscious doctrine. Berkeley and Plato had become for him in his later years influences as intimate as Godwin. Again and again in his later poems, he turns from the cruelties and disappointments of the world, from death and decay and failure, no longer with revolt and anger, but with a serene contempt. Thought is the only reality; time with its appearance of mortality is the dream and the illusion. Says Ahasuerus in *Hellas*:

> The future and the past are idle shadows
> Of thought's eternal flight.

The moral rings out at the end of " The Sensitive Plant " with an almost conversational simplicity ;

> Death itself must be,
> Like all the rest, a mockery.

Most eloquent of all are the familiar lines in *Adonais*:

> 'Tis we who lost in stormy visions keep
> With phantoms an unprofitable strife,

and again :

> The One remains, the many change and pass.
> Heaven's light for ever shines, earth's shadows fly ;
> Life, like a dome of many-coloured glass,
> Stains the white radiance of eternity.

In all the musical and visionary glory of *Hellas* we seem to hear a subtle dialogue. It never reaches a conclusion. It never issues in a dogma. The oracle is dumb, and the end of it all is rather like a prayer. At one moment Shelley toys with the dreary sublimity of the

Stoic notion of world-cycles. The world in the Stoic cosmogony followed its destined course, until at last the elemental fire consumed it in the secular blaze, which became for mediæval Christianity the *Dies irae*. And then once more it rose from the conflagration to repeat its own history again, and yet again, and for ever with an ineluctable fidelity. That nightmare haunts Shelley in *Hellas:*

> Worlds on worlds are rolling ever
> From creation to decay,
> Like the bubbles on a river,
> Sparkling, bursting, borne away.

The thought returns to him in the final chorus like the " motto " of a symphony; and he sings it in a triumphant major key:

> The world's great age begins anew,
> The golden years return,
> The earth doth like a snake renew
> Her winter weeds outworn.
> Heaven smiles, and faiths and empires gleam
> Like wrecks of a dissolving dream.

He is filled with the afflatus of prophecy, and there flow from his lips, as if in improvisation, surely the most limpid, the most spontaneous stanzas in our language:

> A brighter Hellas rears its mountains
> From waves serener far.

He sings happily and, as it were, incautiously of Tempe and Argo, of Orpheus and Ulysses, and then the jarring note of fear is heard:

> O write no more the tale of Troy
> If earth Death's scroll must be,
> Nor mix with Laian rage the joy
> Which dawns upon the free.

He has turned from the empty abstraction of the Godwinian vision of perfection. He dissolves empires and faiths, it is true. But his imagination calls for action and movement. The New Philosophy had driven history out of the picture. This lyrical vision restores it, whole, complete, and literal. The wealth of the concrete takes its revenge upon the victim of abstraction. The men of his golden age are no longer tribeless and nationless. They are Greeks. He has peopled his future; but, as the picture hardens into detail, he seems to shrink from it. That other earlier theme of his symphony recurs. His chorus had sung:

> Revenge and wrong bring forth their kind.
> The foul cubs like their parents are,
> Their den is in their guilty mind,
> And conscience feeds them with despair.

Some end there must be to the *perpetuum mobile* of wrong and revenge. And yet it seems to be in human affairs the very principle of motion. He ends with a cry and a prayer, and a clouded vision. The infinity of evil must be stayed, but what if its cessation means extinction ?

> O cease ! must hate and death return ?
>   Cease ! must men kill and die ?
> Cease ! Drain not to its dregs the urn
>   Of bitter prophecy.
> The world is weary of the past
> O might it die, or rest at last.

Never were there simpler verses in a great song. But he were a bold man who would pretend to know quite certainly what they mean. Shelley is not sure whether his vision of perfection will be embodied in the earth. For a moment he seems to hope that Greece will renew her glories. For one fleeting instant —how ironical the vision seems to us—he conceives that she may be re-incarnated in America. But there is a deeper doubt than this in the prophet's mind. He is not sure that he wants to see the Golden Age founded anew in the perilous world of fact. There is a pattern of the perfect society laid up in Heaven, or if that phrase by familiarity has lost its meaning, let us say rather that the Republic exists firmly founded in the human mind itself :

> But Greece and her foundations are
> Built below the tide of war,
> Based on the crystalline sea
> Of thought and its eternity.

Again, and yet again, he tells us that the heavenly city, the New Athens, " the kingless continents, sinless as Eden " shine in no common day, beside no earthly sea :

> If Greece must be
> A wreck, yet shall its fragments reassemble,
> And build themselves impregnably
> In a diviner clime,
> To Amphionic music on some cape sublime
> Which frowns above the idle foam of Time.

Is it only an eloquent phrase, which satisfies us, by its beautiful words, we know not why, as the chords that make the " full close " in music content us ? Or shall we re-interpret it in our own prose ? Where any mind strives after justice, where any soul suffers and loves and defies, there is the ideal Republic.

We have moved from Dr. Price's sermon to Shelley's chorus. The eloquent old man, preaching in the first flush of hope that came with the new time, conceived that his eyes had seen the great salvation. The day of tyrants and priests was already over, and before the earth closed on his grave, a free Europe would be linked in a confederacy that had abolished war. A generation passed, and the winged victory is now a struggling hope, her pinions singed with the heat of battle, her song mingled with the rumour of massacre, speeding, a fugitive from fact, to the diviner climes of an ideal world. The logic of the revolution has worked to its predestined conclusion. It dreamed too eagerly of the end. It thought in indictments. It packed the present on its tumbrils, and cleared away the past with its dialectical guillotine. When the present was condemned and the past buried, the future had somehow eluded it. It executed the mother, and marvelled that the child should die.

The human mind can never be satisfied with the mere assurance that sooner or later the golden years will come. The mere lapse of time is in itself intolerable. If our waking life and our years of action are to regain a meaning, we must perceive that the process of evolution is itself significant and interesting. We are to-day so penetrated with that thought, that the notion of a state of perfection in the future seems to us as inconceivable and as little interesting as Rousseau's myth of a state of innocence in the past. We know very well that our ideal, whether we see it in the colours of Plato or Godwin or William Morris, does but measure the present development of our faculties. Long before the dream is realised in fact, a new horizon will have been unfolded before the imagination of mankind.

What is of value in this endless process is precisely the unfolding of ideals which record themselves, however imperfectly, in institutions, and still more the developing sense of comradeship and sympathy which links us in relations of justice and love with every creature that feels. We are old enough to pass lightly over the enthusiastic paradoxes that intoxicated the youth of the progressive idea. It is a truth that outworn institutions fetter and dwarf the mind of man. It is also a truth that institutions have moulded and formed that mind. To condemn the past is in the same breath to blast the future. The true basis for that piety towards our venerable inheritance which Burke preached, is that it has made for us the possibility of advance.

But our strivings would be languid, our march would be slow, were it not for the revolutionary leaven which Godwin's generation set fermenting. They taught how malleable and plastic is the human mind. They saw that by a resolute effort to change the environment of institutions and customs which educate us, we can change ourselves. They liberated us not so much from " priests and kings " as from the deadlier tyranny of the belief that human nature, with all its imperfections, is an innate character which it were vain to hope to reform. Their teaching is a tonic to the will, a reminder still eloquent, still bracing, that among the forces which make history the chief is the persuasion of the understanding, the conscious following of a rational ideal. From much that is iconoclastic and destructive in their ideal we may turn away unconvinced. There remain its ardent statement of the duty of humanity, which shames our practice after a century of progress, and its faith in the efficacy of unregimented opinion to supersede brute force. They taught a lesson which posterity has but half learned. We shall be the richer for returning to them, as much by what we reject as by what we embrace.

BIBLIOGRAPHY

GENERAL

LECKY.—*History of England in the 18th Century.*
LESLIE STEPHEN.—*History of English Thought in the 18th Century.*
OLIVER ELTON.—*A Survey of English Literature.*
EDWARD DOWDEN.—*The French Revolution and English Literature.*

The most vivid impression of the period from the standpoint of Godwin's Circle is conveyed in the *Memoirs* of Thomas Holcroft edited by Hazlitt, and in Hazlitt's portraits of Godwin, Malthus and Mackintosh in the *Spirit of the Age* (Everyman's Library).

Of the opposite way of thinking the one immortal record is Burke's *Reflections on the French Revolution.* Lord Morley's *Burke* (English Men of Letters) should be read, and the eloquent exposition by Lord Hugh Cecil (*Conservatism*) in this series.

The main works of the French revolutionary thinkers can be obtained in Dent's series of French classics. For study and pleasure consult Lord Morley's books on Voltaire, Rousseau and Diderot.

The details given in the first chapter concerning the London Corresponding Society are based on its pamphlets in the British Museum.

THOMAS PAINE

Paine's works are published in sixpenny editions by the Rationalist Press, and may be had bound in one volume.

The same press issues a cheap edition of the admirable *Life* by Dr. Moncure D. Conway.

WILLIAM GODWIN

Godwin's works are now procurable only in old libraries, with the exception of *Caleb Williams*. *Political Justice* should be read in the second edition (1796), which is maturer than the first and more lively than the third. A modern summary of it by Mr. Salt, with the full text of the last section " On Property," is published by Swan, Sonnenschein & Co. This selection emphasises his communism, but hardly does full justice to the novelty of his anarchist opinions. Full biographical data are to be found in *William Godwin : His Friends and Contemporaries*, by Mr. Kegan Paul, which contains a readable collection of letters. There is a painstaking and elaborate study in French by Raymond Gourg (Félix Alcan, 1908) and a stimulating little essay in German from the anarchist standpoint (*William Godwin, der Theoretiker des Kommunistischen Anarchismus.* Von Pierre Ramus. Leipsig. Dietrich).

For a modern statement of Anarchist Communism read Kropotkin's *The Conquest of Bread* (Chapman and Hall, 1s.).

MARY WOLLSTONECRAFT

The Rights of Woman has been reissued in the Scott Library (1s.). The volume of *Selections* (2s. 6d.) in the Regent Library (Herbert and Daniel) is well edited by Miss Jebb, and may be recommended, for Mary Wollstonecraft rather gains than loses by compression. For her life Mr. Kegan Paul's *William Godwin* should be consulted. The edition of the *Rights*, published by T. Fisher Unwin, contains an admirable critical study by Mrs. Fawcett. There is no general history of the so-called "feminist" movement, and in English books the French pioneers are ignored. Mr. Lyon Blease has some good historical chapters in *The Emancipation of English Women.*

SHELLEY

Shelley literature is a library in itself. The standard edition is Forman's; the standard biography is the tolerant, human, gossipy *Life* by Professor Dowden. The general reader can use no better edition than Mrs. Shelley's. Of critical essays the most notable are Matthew Arnold's oddly unsympathetic essay, and Sir Leslie Stephen's informing but hostile study on *Godwin and Shelley* ("Hours in a Library"). Professor Santayana may be mentioned among the few critics who have realised that Shelley thought before he sang (*Winds of Doctrine*). Incomparably the best of all the critical essays is the little monograph by Francis Thompson (Burns and Oates).

INDEX

Age of Reason, 75
Arnold, Matthew, 184, 220
Arnot, 174

Baldwin, Edward, 172
Barbauld, Mrs., 192
Blake, Wm., 35, 66
Bright, John, 115
Burke, 15-26, 63
Burney, Fanny, 18

Caleb Williams, 143
Calvinism, 79
Chesterfield, Lord, 195
Clairmont, Mrs. (afterwards Godwin), 169-70
Clairmont, Jane, 169
Coleridge, S. T., 51-55, 86, 156, 173
Condorcet, 22, 23, 27, 92, 109, 110, 197
Convention, English, 44
—— Scottish, 41-43
Cooper, Thomas, 83, 84
Corresponding Society (*see* London)

Dundas, 40, 44

Enquirer, The, 145
Essays (on Religion) by Wm. Godwin, 180

Fénelon, 130
Fleetwood, 176

Gatton, Borough of, 25
Gerrald, Joseph, 43, 88, 89
Gilray, 155
Godwin, William: as historian 22; letter on trial of twelve Reformers, 46; experience during Revolution, 49-51; influence on Coleridge and Southey, 51-55; relation to Paine, 64, 65, 71; relation to Holcroft, 84-88; early life, 78; *Political Justice*, 89-141; Marriage to Mary Wollstonecraft, 149; *Caleb Williams*, 143; controversies, 155; estimate of his work, 163; second marriage and later life, 163; later works, 172; relations with Shelley, 174; death, 178; religious views, 179; intellectual influence on Shelley, 216 *seq.*
Godwin, William (junior), 170
Godwin, Mrs. (*see* Wollstonecraft and Clairmont)

Hardy, Thomas, 33, 37, 39, 41, 44
Hazlitt, 9, 78, 152, 159, 168, 173
Helvétius, 31, 39, 96, 99, 100, 102, 105, 120, 166, 171, 179, 187
Hervé, 119
Holbach, Baron d', 31, 196
Holcroft, Thomas, quoted, 31; early life of, 35, 36; trial of, 44, 45, 48; association with Paine, 65; Influence on Godwin, 84-88

Imlay, Fanny, 148, 169
Imlay, Gilbert, 148

Jones, Sir Wm., 37

Kames, Lord, 193
Kant, 11

Lafayette, 62, 64
Lamb, Charles, 173
Leibnitz, 11, 95
London Corresponding Society, 33-48, 66
Lovell, R., 53
Lytton, Bulwer, 174

Mably, 87

INDEX

Mackintosh, Sir James, 16, 157
Malthus, 29, 158
Margarot, 42
Marius, 128, 220
Milton, 192, 212
Montesquieu, 31, 90, 97
Muir, 42

Napoleon, 154

Paine, Thomas, 16, 34, 39, 56; biographical sketch, 57-68; political views 69-75; religious views, 75-77
Palmer, 42
Pantisocracy, 51-55
Parr, Rev. Dr., 157
Patrickson, 174
Pitt, 40, 44, 66, 91
Plato, Platonism, 102, 104, 126, 131, 197, 218, 234, 243
Plutarch, 182
Political Justice, 89-141
Price, Rev. Dr., 10-15, 248
Priestley, 11, 39, 81, 171

Rights of Man, Paine's, 63, 69
Rights of Woman—a Vindication of the, 148 seq.
Ritson, 35, 170
Roosevelt, Theodore, 75
Rousseau, 21, 101, 191, 194

Sandemanians, 79
Sepulchres, Godwin's Essay on, 22
Shelley, 9, 104, 168; personal relations with Godwin, 174; intellectual outlook, 212; debt to Godwin, 216; his mythology, 225; his view of human perfectibility, 230
Shelley, Mary, née Godwin, 144, 153, 169, 176, 180
Sheridan, 82
Sinclair, 42
Skirving, 42
Socrates, Socratic (*see* Plato)
Southey, 51-55, 151
St. Leon, 160, 172
Stanhope, Earl, 12
Swift, 131, 193

Tolstoy, 120, 138
Tooke, Horne, 34, 43, 44, 46
Turgot, 28

Vindication of the Rights of Women (*see Rights*)
Voltaire, 95, 221

Wedgwood, 170
Weissmann, 98
Wells, H. G., 221
Westbrook, Harriet, 175
Windham, 48
Wollstonecraft, Mary, 16; early life, 147; marriage and death, 149-154; her personality, 202; her originality, 199; summary of "Rights," 204; relation to French Revolution, 186-199; reflection in Shelley, 208
Wordsworth, 8, 51, 157